THE
HEART OF DAVID
JOURNAL

Leading with Vision, Passion and Wisdom

VOLUME 6

By David Mayorga

Published by

SHABAR PUBLICATIONS
www.shabarpublications.com

The Heart of David Journal

Most Shabar Publications products are available at special quantity discounts for bulk purchase for sales promotions, fund-raising and educational needs. For details, write Shabar Publications at mayorga1126@gmail.com.

The Heart of David Volume 6 *by David Mayorga*

Published by Shabar Publications
3833 N. Taylor Rd.
Palmhurst, Texas 78573
www.shabarpublications.com
www.masterbuildertx.com

This book or parts thereof may not be reproduced in any form, stored in a retrieval system, or transmitted in any form by any means - electronic, mechanical, photocopy, recording, or otherwise - without prior written permission of the publisher, except as provided by United States of America copyright law.

Unless otherwise noted, all Scripture quotations are from the New Kings James Version of the Bible. Copyright@1979, 1980, 1982 by Thomas Nelson, Inc., publishers. Used by permission.

Edited by Emily Rose King

Copyright @ 2022 by David Mayorga
All rights reserved

ISBN 978-1-955433-99-0

Volume 6

CONTENTS

Chapter 1: Neither Do I Condemn You! 6

Chapter 2: Be Still and Know! 11

Chapter 3: Overcoming Transgressions, Iniquities, and Sin 14

Chapter 4: Tricked by the Smallest Things 18

Chapter 5: Privileged by His Spirit! 21

Chapter 6: Living in the Fire of His Presence! 24

Chapter 7: The Responsbility of Being Daily Endued! .. 27

Chapter 8: Increased Greatness! 30

Chapter 9: The Need for God's Perspective 35

Chapter 10: Excessively Exalted! 39

Chapter 11: The Secret Behind the Extra Mile! 43

Chapter 12: God Makes It All Happen! 46

Chapter 13: Don't Lose Your Taste! 49

Chapter 14: Can God's Mind Be Changed? 52

Chapter 15: To Those Who Run the Race! 57

Chapter 16: The Author! 61

Chapter 17: Have You Been *Pushed Violently*? 64

Chapter 18: Equipped for this Strange Land! 67

Chapter 19: Continuous Weeping! 70

Chapter 20: The Full Counsel of God 73

Chapter 21: God's Real Pleasure! 77

Chapter 22: The Need for Diligence! 80

Chapter 23: The Immeasurable-ness of God! Part 1 83

Chapter 24: The Immeasurable-ness of God! Part 2 89

Chapter 25: The Immeasurable-ness of God! Part 3 94

Chapter 26: The Immeasurable-ness of God! Part 4 99

Chapter 27: The Immeasurable-ness of God! Part 5 ... 104

Chapter 28: Baptized Into Jesus! 108

Chapter 29: Don't Fool Yourself! 112

Chapter 30: The Move of God! Part 1 116

Chapter 31: The Move of God! Part 2 119

Chapter 32: The Move of God! Part 3 123

Chapter 33: The Move of God! Part 4 128

Chapter 34: The Spirit of Corruption! 132

Chapter 35: How Spiritual Am I? 135

Chapter 36: Beware of Christianity-Lite Part 1 141

Chapter 37: Beware of Christianity-Lite Part 2 145

Chapter 38: Beware of Christianity-Lite Part 3 149

Chapter 39: Glorifying the Father! 152

Chapter 40: God's Atomic Power! Part 1 156

Chapter 41: God's Atomic Power! Part 2 160

Chapter 42: God's Atomic Power! Part 3 163

Chapter 43: God's Atomic Power! Part 4 166

Chapter 44: God's Atomic Power! Part 5 169

Chapter 45: God's Atomic Power! Part 6 172

Chapter 46: God's Atomic Power! Part 7 175

Chapter 47: God's Atomic Power! Part 8 178

Chapter 48: God's Atomic Power! Part 9............. 182

Chapter 49: God's Atomic Power! Part 10 186

Chapter 50: God's Atomic Power! Part 11 189

Chapter 51: God Needs to Get Us There! 192

Chapter 52: In Visions of God! 196

Ministry Information 199

Ministry Resources 200

1

Neither Do I Condemn You!

"But Jesus went to the Mount of Olives. Now early in the morning He came again into the temple, and all the people came to Him; and He sat down and taught them. Then the scribes and Pharisees brought to Him a woman caught in adultery. And when they had set her in the midst, they said to Him, 'Teacher, this woman was caught in adultery, in the very act. Now Moses, in the law, commanded us that such should be stoned. But what do You say?' This they said, testing Him, that they might have something of which to accuse Him. But Jesus stooped down and wrote on the ground with His finger, as though He did not hear. So, when they continued asking Him, He raised Himself up and said to them, 'He who is without sin among you, let him throw a stone at her first.' And again, He stooped down and wrote on the ground. Then those who heard it, being convicted by their conscience, went out one by one, beginning with the oldest even to the last. And Jesus was left alone, and the woman standing in the midst. When Jesus had raised Himself up and saw no one but the woman, He said to her, 'Woman, where are those accusers of yours? Has no one condemned you?' She said, 'No one, Lord.' And Jesus said to her, 'Neither do I condemn you; go and sin no more.' (John 8:1-11)

One of the most powerful Christian truths to ever come down to man from heaven, is regarding the subject of forgiveness. God forgives people their sins, and once forgiven, God never brings it up again. Can you fathom this?

How can a person who has broken God's laws ever find favor with God again? Will God ever look at him or her the same? Will humanity look at that individual who has fallen the same way again?

Well, as far as God goes, He will forgive and restore the wounded heart that has been demolished by sin. His mercy is ever so wide and expands to the deepest valley and goes higher than any mountain. His love is ever-expanding— yes, and His grace continues to give and give.

It is God's heart to touch His creation and restore it! As the Scripture says, **"For God so loved the world that He gave His only begotten Son, that whoever believes in Him should not perish but have everlasting life. For God did not send His Son into the world to condemn the world, but that the world through Him might be saved."** (John 3:16, 17)

Let me just say that many believers don't think like God! No surprise there. An individual without the Spirit of God is the worst, when it comes to forgiving and restoring a fallen soldier. They take on a very strange attitude when it comes to applying the act of forgiving someone who has sinned.

Now the word of God commands us to restore a fallen person; nevertheless, they rather pass judgment and condemn! Listen to Paul here, **"Brothers and sisters, if someone is caught in a sin, you who live by the Spirit should restore that person gently. But watch yourselves, or you also may be tempted."** (Galatians 6:1)

Somehow when forgiveness is not given, something mystical happens. The *law of sowing and reaping* seems to take effect. Suddenly, the person who refused to forgive will find themselves struggling to overcome their own personal sins and struggles. Personally, I am not sure why this happens, but sufficient to say, *What goes around, comes around!*

Ready to Condemn?

Who are those human beings who are ready to condemn other human beings? Where do they come from? Are they perfect and without blame or sinful stains? Could it be that their own sins are not as bad as other people's sins? Can you really measure sin? Are their degrees? Is lying the same as stealing? Is adultery the same as money laundering? Is cheating the same as anger and rage? Is breaking the first commandment as severe as breaking the tenth commandment and vice versa?

My friends, I'm afraid that the commandments of the Lord find all of us human beings guilty before a Holy God. There is no one righteous before God for all have sinned and come short of the glory of God!

Under a Religious Spirit!

The only people who pass judgment are those who are led by a *religious spirit*. Those who feel that they have kept the law without committing any offense against God— well, that is what they think. They see their religious life very differently. They follow God by a standard that God never placed on them. Their sense of holiness is an outward holiness, not a holiness that is offered as worship unto Him. They do their best to keep themselves *pure* from all the ills of the world and all along, they are falling into pride and arrogance.

If the devil cannot make us backslide — he will try to make us front slide!

Where Are Your Accusers?

Before I close this word, I want us to look at one more thing.

The word says, **"When Jesus had raised Himself up and saw no one but the woman, He said to her, 'Woman, where are those accusers of yours? Has no one con-**

demned you?'

She said, 'No one, Lord.'

And Jesus said to her, 'Neither do I condemn you; go and sin no more.'

The accusers were those people who were ready to stone this adulterous woman because she had broken the Law of Moses. They were determined to do it, until the law was applied to their own hearts!

This *religious spirit* will keep believers in bondage, until they start asking themselves the same questions they are asking others!

Before we judge anyone, we should judge ourselves, *Am I breaking the law of God in some way?* If the answer is yes, then we don't qualify to judge; if we have not sinned in any way, shape or form, then we are qualified to throw *the first stone!*

The Scripture says it like this: **"How can you say, 'Brother, let me take the speck out of your eye,' while you yourself fail to see the beam in your own eye? You hypocrite! First take the beam out of your own eye, and then you will see clearly to remove the speck from your brother's eye."** (Luke 6:42) Enough said!

2

Be Still and Know!

"Be still, and know that I *am* God..." (Psalm 46:10a)

While in meditation in the precious *words* of God, I encountered another truth or gold nugget, I should say.

I had always heard these words coming from preachers, friends, and even sang these very words in songs of praise and worship. Yet, as I sang these lyrics, I had very little understanding of this powerful Psalm.

As I took a dive into this portion of Scripture, I learned some valuable lessons. Let me share what God began speaking to me...

For starters, I did a *word study* on this verse. It was this study that opened my eyes and added to my growing revelation of what it means to go deeper into the heart of God.

The words **be still**, are a very powerful set of words. To **be still**, in Hebrew, means **raphah** which means to sink, relax—abandon, become helpless, cease, collapse, to let it go. Also, it means to put an end to a state or an activity.

In this Psalm, the writer says, or suggests to the reader to be still. To take a posture of letting go, to cease trying, to sink and relax. Almost as if to say, *Stop trying to make something happen in human power, it will not get you anywhere!*

He also says in the second part of Psalm 46:10, **"and know."**

Not only to *be still*, but to also know. What does this mean? We already know what it means to *be still*, now let us look at what it means and **know**. ***Know***, in Hebrew means *to get acquainted*.

To get acquainted with the Lord is what God is calling us to do, but first, we must *sink*. *Sinking* speaks of our humility before the Lord. Are you following me?

We cannot rise *in the spirit*, until we learn to *sink the flesh*. The flesh is our soul. This is the place where our human emotions, common sense and feelings exist. It is also known as the house of Satan! Our human soul is what gets seduced by the devil's voice. It is our emotions that often lead us astray!

Our flesh or soul is forever warring against our Spirit (see Galatians 6). It has its own mindset, and it fights against God's mindset. This is the war that wages within us daily!

There is one more Hebrew phrase I want to show you, the phrase, **"I am God."**

The word God here in Hebrew is Elohim, which means God. Also, *the supernatural being who originated and rules over the universe.*

In closing this meditation, here's what I believe God is saying to the reader: Learn to sink (humble) yourself, and at the same time *get acquainted* with *Elohim,* the *God* of the universe who rules everything.

While our soul or flesh sinks (by fasting) we lift our spirit (by personal prayer) to God, so that we may become more acquainted with Him, His ways and His heart!

Neh'enah.

3

Overcoming Transgressions, Iniquities and Sin!

**"Have mercy upon me, O God,
According to Your lovingkindness;
According to the multitude of Your tender mercies,
Blot out my transgressions.
Wash me thoroughly from my iniquity,
And cleanse me from my sin."** (Psalm 51:1, 2)

In this meditation, I want to take you into a deeper realm of what it means to walk under the power of being forgiven by the blood of Jesus.

King David

It was King David who had fallen into the sin of adultery with Bathsheba and later killed this woman's husband to cover his sin. It was by far, not the happiest of moments for King David.

God's Reality Check?

The sins committed by King David are no different than any sin committed by others, with the exception that David's sins brought pain, confusion and even death to others. His sins were *heavy duty* because of the involvement of other people.

It was the Lord who sent Nathan the prophet to speak to David and expose the sin that had been hidden in David's heart for some time. You see, nobody knew about David's sin, but God knew about it.

The exposure of his sin was revealed to the Prophet Nathan, and he went to David's palace and confronted him. It was Psalm 51, that revealed the heart of David's repentance before God.

God's reality checks come to us every time we need to be reminded of who we really are and who God really is! Too often we miss God because we don't keep Him in front of us. We get distracted by the smallest things and we lose sight of what is truly valuable.

Now, as David repented of his sin, he understood that God's tenderness, loving kindness, and mercy were all activated. David knew God, and therefore He could come with an open heart and confess his sin with full assurance that God would hear him.

The Pattern of True Confession

As David begins to make his humble plea with God, he touches on three things. David made mention of *transgressions, iniquity,* and *sin.*

One would think that these are the same thing, but they are not! As a matter of fact, these three follow an order. I will show you...

First, David says in his prayer of repentance to God, **"Blot out my transgressions."**

It is important to know what a transgression is before we can repent of it. Would you agree? Transgression comes from the Hebrew word ***pesha*** which means *breach of trust*— or *a rebellious act*. Also, it can mean *a violation of a law, duty, or moral principle.*

It was important for David to tell himself that he had violated a law— a moral principle. God knew that, but David needed to say that to himself in the presence of God. Unless we are willing to confess our *transgressions*, they will remain on us!

Secondly, David prayed, **"Wash me thoroughly from my iniquity..."**

What is an iniquity? The Hebrew word for *iniquity* is **avon,** which means *guilty*. The *feeling of guilt* after one commits a transgression, is a very powerful emotion that hurts to the core of your human spirit. David knew all too well that his spirit had been damaged by his transgression. Do you follow?

Finally, David pleaded with God in prayer with these words: **"And cleanse me from my sin."**

The key word here is *sin*. The word *sin* in Hebrew comes from the word **chattaah** which means *sinful thing*. Also, *it's an act or feeling that transgresses something forbidden or ignores something required by God's law or character; whether in thought, feeling, speech, or action.*

It was enough for David to know that something *required by God's law or character* had been transgressed by him. David was pleading with the Lord to cleanse him from the sin of breaking God's heart for doing what he did.

In our walk with God, we must learn to truly repent before the Lord when we fall short of His expectations. It would be of great value if we learned the steps to confess *King David's* way. Acknowledging that we have broken God's heart is enough, but undoing the transgression and removing the iniquity will play a huge role in our restoration process.

Neh'enah.

4

Tricked by the Smallest Things!

**"Catch us the foxes,
The little foxes that spoil the vines,
For our vines have tender grapes."**
(Song of Solomon 2:15)

While going for my daily run at the park, I had a tremendous experience with God; one of those experiences that can possibly be a *game-changer* in one's life! I felt moved by His Spirit to share this insight with you. Let God speak to you as you read:

While running in the morning, about 6am, I came to my final stretch, super tired and all, I decided to try running on a new sidewalk that had been built at a park near my house. It was new, it was nice, it was well lit, and I didn't think twice about running on it.

I did notice that the sidewalk had been nicely crafted as it swerved around the big oak trees on the path. While I came around on the sidewalk that goes around an oak tree, I did not notice that at the bottom of the oak tree, there was part of a root that had been dug out, but not removed fully. So it was sticking up, like a trap waiting for someone to run close to it—it was there as if to cause someone to stumble. The root must have been about 3 inches tall. Well, that *someone* was me!

As tired as I was from my long run, I came around that sidewalk and got close to that oak tree to the point that my left tennis shoe hit the 3-inch root, and down I went! My knee got badly scraped on the concrete and my face hit the ground which was all mud. I was so embarrassed by the fall. Has this ever happened to you? It probably has, but you won't say!

Let me tell you, I learned a great deal from this.

The first thing I learned was that when one is weary, fatigued, and extremely tired, it is wiser to stop doing what one is doing and find a place to rest. This is not only good advice but valuable wisdom.

In our spiritual walk in the Lord, one must recognize that when one is fatigued, faith leaves! When one makes the attempt to make important decisions, *weariness* will cloud the mind and fatigue will *pollute* the heart with *carnal choices*. It would be wise to never make valuable decisions when in a state of *weariness* and *fatigue!*

The second thing I learned was how even small things can bring one down! I didn't have to run into the oak tree to kiss the floor— all it took to bring me down was a 3-inch piece of root bark! How about that?

Too often, we tend to be so self-reliant, arrogant, and full of pride (which is the enemy's attitude against God) that we are tricked by the smallest things. We say to ourselves— *it will not hurt me*, or *it will not hurt anyone else*, or *I can find my way out of this*. Is anyone guilty of doing this? Think about it.

In the Song of Solomon 2:15, the Bible talks about the *little foxes* spoiling the vine. Do foxes like grapes? If they do, I didn't know that. Well, the fact is that *little foxes* are more about destroying the vine than eating the grapes. They love to gnaw at the trunk, and dig around the vine to expose the root, eat the grapes, and finally leave it in ruins.

We must keep these *words of wisdom*, heralding loudly, before us. The greatest of people have been brought down by the smallest things. Let us keep on guard for those little foxes that want to spoil our vine!

Neh'enah.

5

Privileged by His Spirit!

**"Blessed is the man You choose,
And cause to approach You,
That he may dwell in Your courts."** (Psalm 65:4)

When we speak of being privileged, I have my doubts that many people do not understand what it truly means to be privileged. Before I dig any deeper into this word, I want to give you the definition of what the word privilege means.

In Webster's Dictionary, the word privilege, means *a right/immunity granted as a peculiar benefit, advantage, or favor.*

One would think that most everyone has been granted certain benefits in life— many have advantages or have been shown favor by others like parents, bosses, political leaders, or simply just another friend. Though this may be true in many cases, it doesn't necessarily mean that everyone is favored or privileged by the Lord!

Let me also say this as a side note: *If* and *when* the Lord moves our hearts to *draw near,* we better get ready for a tremendous amount of events to be set in motion in us and around us — for this is a sign that God will be moving!

The Blessed Man: Why Was He Chosen?

As far as I can remember, I have always believed that God favors or releases certain advantages to those who favor Him! The Scripture above says, **"Blessed is the man You choose…"**

My question is: How did God choose that man? What gave this man *the edge* and provided him this highly coveted spot?

I wholeheartedly believe that this spot is given to those who choose God, who favor God, who understand *the value* of being privileged by the Lord. I seriously believe that to the degree that we embrace God, He will embrace us. There is a Scripture in the Book of James that bears this truth out: **"Draw near to God and He will draw near to you."** (James 4:8a).

We should always react *in faith* to take the first step toward God in every circumstance.

Invited!

Secondly, we find that God will stir man's heart to *approach* Him. This doesn't come from a natural desire in us. It must be the Lord— the One who does the inviting first. It takes God to know God! We then get to respond to such a glorious invitation.

Now, I don't believe that there is a greater privilege than being invited into the presence of God. It almost seems like a hand-picked invitation to a special banquet.... doesn't this sound familiar?

In His Courts

Finally, the Lord has privileged us to be in His courts. Those whom He favors will experience the secrets of the Lord. For the Lord Himself will reveal His heart, His mind, His plans, and anything that will be of great value to that servant.

To be privileged by being personally invited to be in the courts of God has to be one of the most rewarding experiences for all who choose God first– those who make the Lord their number one priority!

Neh'enah.

6

Living in the Fire of His Presence!

**"As wax melts before the fire,
So let the wicked perish at the presence of God."** (Psalm 68:2)

Many Scriptures describe God's presence as *fire*. As a matter of fact, *fire* is also a symbol of the Holy Spirit.

God's presence is like a fire when it moves inside the human heart and bones. If you have never experienced the fire of God's presence, all one must do is ask God to touch you with it.

In my search for God's touch, I discovered that when the fire is burning within me—I know, and I also know when the fire is absent.

I meditated intently on this Psalm to know more about the fire of God. The writer makes a figurative comparison using *wax melting before the fire*. Obviously, fire melts wax, just like when a candle is burning. The bigger the flame, the hotter the feeling. The wider the fire, the more territory that can *potentially* burn. The degree of how much fire is present — is the degree of its burning!

Jesus: The Light of the World!

Jesus said in John 8:12, **"I am the light of the world. He who follows Me shall not walk in darkness but have the light of life."**

The light here is the result of a lamp burning. In essence, this is what I believe the Lord was trying to say to His disciples: *I am like a lamp that lights the way, so that people may see and then follow the right path in their lives.*

Anyone can figure out that the brighter the flame in a lamp is, the greater the light. If there is greater light — then a wider path to walk on or run in is made available. Light is dependent upon the amount of fire in the lamp. The more fire — the brighter the flame!

How Much Fire is In You?

Now, the real question is — how much fire (God's presence) is in you? How bright is it? Can you evaluate and *honestly* see where you are going in life? If you are confused, if you are lost, if you don't know where you are headed, if you are doubting, or if you are fearful — my suggestion to you (and perhaps the wisest answer anyone can give you) is to *turn on the light!*

The Enemy Loves the Dark!

It is in the *dark places* that the enemy loves to come and hide; this is the place where he establishes his strongholds. When we walk in darkness, we will eventually stumble, we all do — guaranteed! It is when we fail, that the enemy steps in and takes advantage of our failure. The enemy then proceeds to control and manipulate our life through guilt and shame.

Once you ask God to forgive you for your sins and get washed in the blood of Jesus, you will feel His fire and light start to burn again. Once the burning starts, the enemy will run for cover! This is why the Psalm says, **"As wax melts before the fire, So let the wicked perish at the presence of God."**

As I close, let me encourage you to keep the fire burning in your soul. Allow God to have the first place in your life always. Seek His face daily; walk in His counsel daily, and set yourself on fire with the fire of God— then invite the enemy to come and see you burn! See if he opens your invitation and comes.

Neh'enah.

7

The Responsibility of Being Daily Endued!

"Behold, I send the Promise of My Father upon you; but tarry in the city of Jerusalem until you are endued with power from on high." (Luke 24:49)

"But put on the Lord Jesus Christ, and make no provision for the flesh, to *fulfill* its lusts." (Romans 13:14)

A Visitation from the Lord

I want to open these thoughts with the definition of the word *endued*. The word *endued* means to be or become bestowed or endowed with a quality or condition— understood as being wrapped in a covering.

It was in the days before Pentecost, that Christ ordered His disciples not to leave Jerusalem. He ordered them to stay and to remain in the city of Jerusalem until they would be *endued* or *clothed* in power.

The enduement of power, would be all that the disciples needed to make a world impact with the gospel of the kingdom of God.

Daily Enduements!

Now, not only did this power work for the disciples of old, but it works for the disciples and close followers of Jesus today! For some reason, many believe that this power is no longer available today. Some even believe that Christ no longer heals supernaturally anymore.

If the disciples saw the grave need for this awesome enduement of power *yesterday*, how much more in dire need are we of this power *today*?

Continue Putting Christ On

As I meditated upon the word of God in Romans, I discovered something very interesting. I discovered the words of the Apostle Paul when he said, **"But put on the Lord Jesus Christ, and make no provision for the flesh, to *fulfill* its lusts."**

Too often we are instructed to fill ourselves with the Spirit of God– to wait until we are clothed with power to serve and do great exploits for God, yet we do very little waiting to overcome personal secrets or open sin.

In Romans 13:14, the Apostle Paul uses the same word *endued* or *clothed* when he says, **"But put on the Lord Jesus Christ…"**

The words *put on* are the same words used when it says, **"till you be *endued* with power…"**

In other words, we must continue to get clothed with Christ not only for service, but also for holy living. We need the thoughts of God to know what we are doing and where we are going as a church!

We must not only *put on* Christ, but also, we cannot make provisions for the flesh to fulfill its lust. Our responsibility grows as we don't *only* get clothed with more of Jesus, but also, we must be strong and stay away from things that will feed our flesh and bring us to fulfill wicked desires, leading us ultimately to death!

Why Do I Need to Be Endued Daily?

My conclusion is this: I need to be endued daily for the simple reason that I need God's fire in my bones for the sake of advancing the message of the kingdom of God. Secondly, I need to be endued so that I may live an exemplary life of passion and zeal before God and man.

Neh'enah.

8

Increased Greatness!

"You, **who have shown me great and severe troubles, Shall revive me again, And bring me up again from the depths of the earth. You shall increase my greatness, And comfort me on every side."** (Psalm 70:20-21)

A journey with God has been one of the most exciting ventures ever revealed to mankind! Without doubt, I believe that God has equipped all of us who believe in such a journey filled with highways full of potholes, rough terrain, and sometimes smooth roads, I said, *sometimes...*

For some reason, the life of the Apostle Paul comes to mind here, when he wrote part of his journey in God to the Corinthian church in 1 Corinthians 4:9-13. Just read this: **"For I think that God has displayed us, the apostles, last, as men condemned to death; for we have been made a spectacle to the world, both to angels and to men. We** *are* **fools for Christ's sake, but you** *are* **wise in Christ! We** *are* **weak, but you** *are* **strong! You** *are* **distinguished, but we** *are* **dishonored! To the present hour we both hunger and thirst, and we are poorly clothed, and beaten, and homeless. And we labor, working with our own hands. Being reviled, we bless; being persecuted, we endure; being**

defamed, we entreat. We have been made as the filth of the world, the offscouring of all things until now."

The Power of a New Life

As we have come to the realization that Jesus is the Way, the Truth, and the Life, we have also entered into His life. His life is characterized by commitment, humility, passion, and sacrifice. None of these attributes are practiced without a high price paid. To be a man or a woman of God, one must learn to pay the price to earn these characteristics.

What exactly do I mean by a price paid for these characteristics? What I mean is this: unless we are willing to die to *self*, to neglect self and to carry His cross daily, it will be impossible to *walk out* these spiritual qualities.

Remember: The flesh hates to submit to God, and it won't unless we crucify it. So the walk is not an easy breezy one. Something must die — it is you! Unless you die, you can't resurrect in Christ's power to live out this blessed life He calls us to.

Personal Failures

In the journey with God, a servant will face many personal challenges. The longing cry in our flesh which is latent in us, will be heard. The desire to please the flesh and forsake the truth of God, will forever be heard till the day we pass on from this life and be with our King forever!

One must always keep close to Jesus in their walk and not neglect the personal time of prayer and devotion to God. Rather, skip sleep instead of missing an appointment of sweet communion with Jesus!

Life's Challenges

As we venture through our journey, we will be faced by many things. Our whole being will be challenged, not just a specific area. This is what I call *God's Workshop!* In other words: Is God working on you?

Paul was working on the great Apostle Paul— just read this: "**. . . in labors more abundant, in stripes above measure, in prisons more frequently, in deaths often. From the Jews five times I received forty *stripes* minus one. Three times I was beaten with rods; once I was stoned; three times I was shipwrecked; a night and a day I have been in the deep; in journeys often, *in* perils of waters, *in* perils of robbers, *in* perils of *my own* countrymen, in perils of the Gentiles, *in* perils in the city, *in* perils in the wilderness, *in* perils in the sea, *in* perils among false brethren; in weariness and toil, in sleeplessness often, in hunger and thirst, in fastings often, in cold and nakedness—besides the other things, what comes upon me daily: my deep concern for all the churches."** (1 Corinthians 11:23-28)

God will always find a way to test His vessels and bring out the sweetest honey out of them by using adversity. Sometimes adversity comes from the outside, and often, it comes from within us. Whatever the case may be with you and I, God will be glorified through all of it!

Increased Greatness!

After we have been tested, tried, and fried— the Lord will revive us again; yes, He will *resurrect* us from the earth with a new form, a new design, and a heart full of expectation!

Here's what the Psalmist said about this:

**"*You*, who have shown me great and severe troubles,
Shall revive me again,
And bring me up again from the depths of the earth."**

During our winter this year, we experienced some frigid weather in February. I don't believe we had seen such cold temperatures in our region in a very long time.

As a result of the freezing weather, most plants died or went into hibernation. They simply got burned by the icy cold temperature and just died!

Our personal tests are very much like this. They [the tests] come and kill everything on the surface, so that the roots may go deeper in search for nutrients to survive. Once the freeze is over, the plant begins to sprout again in a more beautiful, refined form. I have seen this in my own flower garden. Thank God for the resurrection process!

Finally, greatness appears!

**"You shall increase my greatness,
And comfort me on every side."**

Here's what the test produces in us. Initially, the test brings about death. After death does its perfect work, the resurrection process begins. It is at this stage of the process that new life begins to sprout forth. Without doubt, there will be newness coming forth and along with it, bring comfort on so many levels.

There is no need for the servant of God to panic, to jump ship, to criticize, to run away, or to blame the situation at hand —you must know that it is the Lord, bringing about *increased greatness* to you, in you, and through you!

Neh'enah.

Volume 6

9

The Need for God's Perspective!

"Behold, these *are* the ungodly,
Who are always at ease;
They increase *in* riches.
Surely I have cleansed my heart *in* vain,
And washed my hands in innocence.
For all day long I have been plagued,
And chastened every morning.
If I had said, 'I will speak thus,'
Behold, I would have been untrue to the generation of Your children.
When I thought *how* to understand this,
It *was* too painful for me—
Until I went into the sanctuary of God;
Then I understood their end." (Psalm 73:12-17)

In meditating upon this revelation that the Lord showed me early today, I want to bring forth a very common situation that happens or has happened to all believers. This very thing that I am talking about will affect our spirit, our soul, and eventually our body. Just open your heart and ponder the following words.

In the Psalm written here, the writer makes a plea to God for how wicked and evil people seem to get away with evil doing. It almost seems that they don't get punished for all that they do. This includes the people they hurt, the people they betray, the people they steal from, those they abuse mentally, emotionally, and even physically! There is so much injustice; it all seems unfair!

The writer goes on to say, **"**(evil doers) **are always at ease; they increase in riches. Surely I have cleansed my heart in vain."**

He makes the comparison to the wicked by saying, **"I have cleansed my heart in vain, and washed my hand in innocence."**

Do you see the unfairness here? Do you see how it can make someone who makes every effort to be Christlike feel when others seem to *get away with murder!*

The Scripture states that the wicked even, **"increase in riches."**

Wow. How can this be? Instead of them being punished for the pain they cause, they get richer! Amazing!

Yet in all the unfairness we see with our natural eyes, and the things we hear with our natural ears, our judgment is incomplete at best. God doesn't see the way we see things; He doesn't hear things the way we do!

To get a good idea of what God is *actually* thinking, we must ascend to the throne where He dwells. Once there, we will get a glimpse of how God really sees the wicked.

Everything is Different in the Sanctuary (Presence) of God!

**"When I thought how to understand this,
It was too painful for me—
Until I went into the sanctuary of God;
Then I understood their end."**

The Psalmist had all these ill feelings welling up inside him that became bothered and even sick from thinking of the unfairness. When we fail to see things from God's perspective, it can potentially damage our spirit, soul, and body. Yes, even to the point of getting extremely sick from it.

The good thing is that everything changed when the Psalmist said, **"It was too painful for me – until I went into the sanctuary of God; then I understood their end."**

Seeing life with our natural faculties can be very disheartening, disappointing, and even disgraceful! We must see with the eyes of God. The only way to do this, is to ascend to the throne room in full surrender with a worshipful heart and inquire of the Lord to see what is truly happening in the situations that surround us.

The answer to life's difficulties can be solved when we get a clear view of how God sees things around us— then we can process correctly.

Neh'enah.

Volume 6

10

Excessively Exalted?

"And to keep me from being puffed up *and* **too much elated by the exceeding greatness** (preeminence) **of these revelations, there was given me a thorn** (a splinter) **in the flesh, a messenger of Satan, to rack** *and* **buffet** *and* **harass me, to keep me from being excessively exalted. Three times I called upon the Lord** *and* **besought** [Him] **about this and begged that it might depart from me; But He said to me, My grace** (My favor and loving-kindness and mercy) **is enough for you** (sufficient against any danger and enables you to bear the trouble) **for *My* strength** *and* **power are made perfect** (fulfilled and completed) *and* **show themselves most effective in** [your] **weakness. Therefore, I will all the more gladly glory in my weaknesses** *and* **infirmities, that the strength** *and* **power of Christ** (the Messiah) **may rest** (yes, may pitch a tent over and dwell) **upon me!"** (2 Corinthians 12: 7-9)

Years ago, I came across a small pamphlet that challenged me in the most profound of ways; the inscription on the front cover of this pamphlet had this in bright blue letters, *"Others May, You Cannot!"*

After reading this pamphlet a few times, I concluded that true servants of the Lord are like no other. They are different in every way. They think, act, and process with a different perspective; they not only see things from God's perspective, but they *literally live* under different marching orders. They march to the beat of a different drummer if you will. Their philosophy of life is filtered through the wisdom and knowledge of God; yes, their lives are not their own.

Why am I writing on this subject today? The reason for my writing comes from what I keep hearing repeatedly from *so-called* believers who hang out in a building at 11am on Sundays only!

They make every effort to hear a 20-minute sermon, but with no real intent to hear and experience God; they are content to live their lives free from engaging God through the Holy Spirit, they settle for a religious gathering without power!

Power Comes from a Life of Brokenness!

It is evident to me that much of what we hear from pulpits today is nothing but empty words; words that only tickle people's ears and pamper their flesh. No power in the pulpit means no power in the pew!

Is it any wonder why we still struggle to get our act together in our walk with God? Is it any wonder why the gospel hasn't been preached in all the world yet?

As much as many want to blame a vicious devil as the culprit for our spiritual poverty, let this truth be settled in our hearts: *Much of our personal struggle has to do with an undeveloped and uncultured spiritual life.*

Our Pampered Age!

Too many believers have been sold a gospel that caters to their flesh; it accommodates believers to their wants and carnal desires. A gospel that doesn't require any commitment in both our personal and ministry walk has been pretty much the order of the day in our religious world!

Becoming a Man of Power!

Paul was a man of power because he allowed God to have His way in his life. It was God who kept Paul in check! Paul experienced great revelations from the Lord; he saw incredible visions from heaven and had understanding like few had ever seen.

Yet in all his wonderful experiences, Paul was not allowed to share most of them. Paul was vexed by continuous opposition in his life. Paul made mention of this when he said, **"And to keep me from being puffed up and too much elated by the exceeding greatness** (preeminence) **of these revelations, there was given me a thorn** (a splinter) **in the flesh, a messenger of Satan, to rack** *and* **buffet** *and* **harass me, to keep me from being excessively exalted."**

(1 Corinthians 12:7)

If there is one thing, I have truly grasped in my walk with the Lord is this: If God truly cares about me and loves me like He says He does – then He will always make sure that I stay humble walking in brokenness. It may not be your flavor of understanding , but God will not allow His man or woman (servants) to be given to pride, arrogance, and fleshly desires for long.

God will allow something or someone to put you in your place! This is God's method. You might think it is not fair; you might even pray and cry out saying, *It is not fair God that you are taking me through this!* But in all our whining, we will hear God say, either softly or loudly: **"Others May, You Cannot!"**

Neh'enah.

11

The Secret Behind the Extra Mile!

"You have heard that it was said, *'An eye for an eye and a tooth for a tooth.'*

But I tell you not to resist an evil person. But whoever slaps you on your right cheek, turn the other to him also. If anyone wants to sue you and take away your tunic, let him have your cloak also. And whoever compels you to go one mile, go with him two." (Matthew 5:38-41)

Here are some things to ponder. As I meditated today, the Spirit of the Lord caused me to see this one particular idea in this verse. I heard the Spirit of God say to me, *David, as you live out your life— you will always have to deal with the two natures: your flesh and my Spirit within you.*

Most believers truly don't know how to walk in the spirit of the Lord. As a matter of fact, most believers make the most noble and humble attempts to walk and please God, but it is in their own power. The very second someone crosses them, or criticizes them, or does something mean to them— their fleshly nature comes out and totally destroys the testimony of who Jesus is within them.

People around us who don't know the Lord are watching

intently to see if we are the real deal or if we are just pretending to be something we are not. They can tell if we are *playing church* or some religious game.

The Real Test

The real test of every believer comes when he or she must step out from the comfort of what they know into the unknown, or from being used to doing the bare minimum and nothing more than that!

The mark of true servanthood is not based on the little you do. Recompense comes when you go above and beyond what you can do. Most people give money to the church with a tight hand (not wanting to let it go). This kind of grudgeful giving is exactly what I am talking about.

Take for instance the homeless man who lives under the bridge. He gets out every morning with his sign and money bag to collect from cars that come to the stop light. Most people will only give him spare change, but not a considerable amount— not even a few dollars to buy a decent meal.

The idea of helping people in need is a great and godly idea, yet when it comes to releasing a full blessing, we have a hard time pouring it out to those we don't know. We can think of a million excuses of why we don't want to do this, yet, Jesus said, *go extra!*

Flesh versus Spirit!

We all don't usually have a hard time buying a cupcake or two from the little girl that stops by the restaurant where we are having dinner. She goes from table to table hoping to land a sale and collect some money for her mother who is dying of cancer at home.

Now, if the Spirit of the Lord said to you, *Stop! Don't buy cupcakes! Give her $100.00 dollars right now!* I have blessed you abundantly with health, wealth, and My sweet presence. Don't you dare give them $1.00 for those cupcakes… shame on you!

You see the first part is *flesh*, (the first mile is on us, our fleshly love, care, and compassion) and the second part has to be done by His Spirit in us (this would be the second mile that Jesus spoke of).

As I close this meditation, what is the Lord speaking to our hearts?

Here is what I believe God is saying: When we help someone cross a street, the idea of helping them is a great one, yet in all our help, God may ask us to not only help them cross the street, but to also give them some money for a good meal!

Neh'enah.

12

God Makes It All Happen!

**"For the Lord God is a sun and shield;
The Lord will give grace and glory;
No good *thing* will He withhold
From those who walk uprightly."** (Psalm 84:11)

Dwelling in His awesome presence this morning, I came across this one verse in Psalm 84. It opened a fresh understanding of God's greatness and concern over my life as well. Let me share some insight with you.

The first thing I read was how the Lord Himself is both sun and shield. In other words, the Lord provides sun for those who love the sun, but also provides shields for those who think it might be too hot. No one is left out in God's economy. He does all things perfect and at the same time beautiful! Have you found this to be true in your own life?

As I meditated deeper into this one truth, I also realized that God does not withhold anything good from me. He will always be attentive to my heart's desires and will move accordingly in His time to bless me in due time!

One thing to understand as one of God's servants is that whatever God sets in motion in my life or around me, God has all the steps to it. I should never worry about my future if God and I are in good standing. He will help me to understand anything I don't or can't see or understand.

He Starts All Things!

One sure thing about the Lord is this: He always begins with the intent to complete what He has in mind. He never leaves us alone wondering if we are going to get to the finish line. He always guides us in the right path and by His grace and power— gets us to His desired end!

I think too many times, believers wonder why things take too long to *materialize*. Others wonder if God has forgotten them and left them inside a fiery furnace to burn. The answer to all these questions is that God started something in us, and we can rest assured that He will also complete it!

Christ is the First and the Last!

In Revelation 1:11, Jesus said, **"I am the Alpha and the Omega, the First and the Last."**

What this means is that Christ is the founder and developer of everything. He gives an idea, He cultivates the idea, He releases the ability to carry-out the idea, He sustains the idea, He makes the idea materialize, and finally, He makes the idea stand by His own power.

The Lord is the *First* to initiate. He draws us to Himself and then speaks to us; He then proceeds to show us what He wants from us, or He might just have a simple task for us to follow.

He is the *Last* because He will be exalted and glorified by our obedience to Him. In the end of our lives, or at the close of a project, Christ will be glorified by it all!

Let me just close this mediation by saying that whatever God allows in our lives, He has all the pieces and steps to this thing we call a mysterious puzzle!

Neh'enah.

13

Don't Lose Your Taste!

"I have been crucified with Christ; it is no longer I who live, but Christ lives in me…" (Galatians 2:20a)

"Now therefore, it is already an utter failure for you that you go to law against one another. Why do you not rather accept wrong? Why do you not rather *let yourselves* be cheated?" (1 Corinthians 6:7)

As we walk with God, protecting our testimony becomes our priority, and we become more conscious about our thoughts, words, and actions.

I'm very aware that we, as believers, go through rough patches in life. Not all days are rainbows and sunshine! As you well know, adversity can have the potential to wreck, perhaps not your life, but your day or week, depending on your response to the predicament. This forever will be a challenge for you and me.

Handling ourselves under duress is one tough challenge; I mean, we don't need an audience to see our weaknesses, but oftentimes we do have an audience. This audience that I am referring to might be family, friends, acquaintances, or just people passing by.

Being Watched!

I have had the experience of being around people when I was challenged to decide under pressure. Let me share this story: I was in the middle of a home Bible study, when suddenly a loud bang was heard. *What was that?* said one of the brothers at the study. I quickly jumped up and went outside. My new car had been vandalized at about 8pm; someone passed by my house and threw a brick at the windshield. Ouch!

In all the years I had lived at this address, nothing like this had ever happened before— not to me or my property or anyone around me for that matter. I was stunned.

As I looked out and waited for the police to arrive, all my guests at the Bible study were watching me carefully. What were they looking at? They were looking and wondering if what I truly believed in my heart, *aligned* with my actions. My thoughts, my words, and my actions were now in full display.

Finally, one of my guests *stepped-out in faith* and asked me, *Pastor David, what do you think about all this?* I remember my answer up to this day, almost as if it happened last night: After taking a deep breath, I said, *Perhaps the Lord allowed this to test me in my thoughts, words and deeds — for the sake of you little ones (referring to my young disciples). God will take care of this in the most spectacular way!* I concluded.

God did.

Now, what if I had allowed my *old self* to take over? What if I started to curse and had *damned* this and that and those who did the deed? Can you imagine my followers? What would they think of their wicked and damning pastor? It would not have glorified Christ at all!

How many times have we found ourselves in similar situations? Our audience can vary, it might be your own children, or your parents. How will you react? What will we allow to come out of us? Will our thoughts, words, and actions glorify the King of Glory?

Your Testimony is Salt!

"You are the salt of the earth; but if the salt has become tasteless, how can it be made salty *again*? It is no longer good for anything, except to be thrown out and trampled underfoot by people." (Matthew 5:13)

Don't lose your saltiness; don't become tasteless — for how will you become salty again? This speaks of our testimony before people. Protect your flavor and use it to make others thirsty for God.

Neh'enah.

14

Can God's Mind Be Changed?

"They forgot God their Savior,
Who had done great things in Egypt,
Wondrous works in the land of Ham,
Awesome things by the Red Sea.
Therefore He said that He would destroy them,
Had not Moses His chosen one stood before Him in the breach,
To turn away His wrath, lest He destroy *them*." (Psalm 106:21-23)

In studying and meditating on this particular subject, I'm reminded of how kind, loving, and compassionate God really is. As a matter of fact, one Scripture says that God doesn't punish us as we should be punished. All of us can attest to that!

While reading Psalm 106, I came across these events that the Hebrew children had to deal with, as they were struggling to come out of Egypt. If you remember, it was God who raised up Moses as a deliverer; it was Moses who by the hand of God performed great signs and wonders in the land of Egypt. It was Moses, God's servant, who confronted Pharaoh and then released the ten plagues over the land.

So far, it has been all God using His servant Moses to do the miraculous work that would eventually release the Hebrew children from Egyptian bondage.

Then it came to pass that Pharaoh released the Hebrew children to go into the wilderness and worship Jehovah. If you remember, no sooner had they been released from bondage, that Pharaoh went back on his word and started to pursue the Hebrew children and try to bring them back. It was too late!

The children of Israel were already crossing the Red Sea on dry ground and once again, God performed another wonder!

As they crossed over, they celebrated with song and dance. They were joyful, they were happy, they were thrilled that God had done this great work, thus they worshiped continually— but for how long did this emotion last?

When the Emotion Dies!

When the emotion dies, true faith must kick in! If there is no faith activated, only emotions of sadness and discouragement will remain. What once was vibrant is now dead! What was once a motivation, will now become only a powerless memory!

After losing their high-energy emotion, here's what followed:

**"They forgot God their Savior,
Who had done great things in Egypt,
Wondrous works in the land of Ham,
Awesome things by the Red Sea."**

Is this not tragic? Is this not a very sad situation? Once enlightened by Jehovah God and His servant Moses, the children of Israel have no memory of who God is, and what God did through Moses. Isn't that something?

How does God respond to something like this? Is God hurt? Does He feel betrayed? What will God do to His creation when His creation pays Him back with unbelief and negligence? Read on:

**"Therefore He said that He would destroy them,
Had not Moses His chosen one stood before Him in the breach,
To turn away His wrath, lest He destroy *them*."**

As a result of their waywardness, God set Himself to destroy His own people! There comes a time when God judges severely; I'm sure it's not one of God's first choices, but eventually God will lay down the law and punish accordingly and justly!

Moses Intercedes!

Whether our personal theology provides a specific teaching that alludes to God changing His mind or not, Psalm 106 says that God's mind can be changed— Moses did it!

Moses stood before the Lord and made a plea for God's people: See how it all came to pass: **"And the Lord said to Moses, 'Go, get down! For your people whom you brought out of the land of Egypt have corrupted** *themselves.* **They have turned aside quickly out of the way which I commanded them. They have made themselves a molded calf, and worshiped it and sacrificed to it, and said, "This is your god, O Israel, that brought you out of the land of Egypt!"'**

And the Lord said to Moses, 'I have seen this people, and indeed it is a stiff-necked people! Now therefore, let Me alone, that My wrath may burn hot against them and I may consume them. And I will make of you a great nation.'

Then Moses pleaded with the Lord his God, and said: 'Lord, why does Your wrath burn hot against Your people whom You have brought out of the land of Egypt with great power and with a mighty hand? Why should the Egyptians speak, and say, "He brought them out to harm them, to kill them in the mountains, and to consume them from the face of the earth? Turn from Your fierce wrath, and relent from this harm to Your people. Remember Abraham, Isaac, and Israel, Your servants, to

whom You swore by Your own self, and said to them, "I will multiply your descendants as the stars of heaven; and all this land that I have spoken of I give to your descendants, and they shall inherit *it* **forever."'**

So the Lord relented from the harm which He said He would do to His people." (Exodus 32:7-14)

If you see this situation, whether it be in your life or the life of someone else, plead before the Lord for their sake. I know that sometimes people can be mean and deserve to be punished— but really, who are we to release judgment on another?

Pray and intercede to the Lord! Who knows if He will show mercy and favor on us— in spite of us!

Neh'enah.

15

To Those Who Run the Race!

"Do you not know that those who run in a race all run, but one receives the prize? Run in such a way that you may obtain it. And everyone who competes for the prize is temperate in all things. Now they *do it* to obtain a perishable crown, but we *for* an imperishable crown. Therefore, I run thus: not with uncertainty. Thus, I fight: not as one who beats the air. But I discipline my body and bring it into subjection, lest, when I have preached to others, I myself should become disqualified." (1 Corinthians 9:24-27)

In these verses, the Apostle Paul brings about an interesting subject: The runner's attitude while racing. He also brings forth an intriguing perspective from a runner's point of view— yes, and probably a viewpoint that stems from a philosophy of winning.

As I meditated over and over on this present truth, I realized that there is a secret to winning. The secret rests upon the fact that as you make it your aim to compete for a prize, whether you win the prize or not, you are still a winner if you learn how to be *temperate in all things*. Let me explain to you what the Spirit of God is saying here:

Running in Such a Way!

First, we must realize that our lives are a race, spiritually speaking. We are all running the race to win an imperishable crown. Many people who run in races, often run against obstacles: they might give up, get injured, or lose the passion to finish, etc.

There are various reasons why too many don't get to the finish line. I am sure you have seen this on TV watching the Olympic races, or perhaps a competition at the local high school or college. There is always one person who crosses the finish line first. Yes, the winner is awarded the prize, but what got them to that place? Let us see...

The Apostle Paul speaks of runners who run in races but only one of them wins the prize— why? Or better said, how did he beat everyone else? I am sure they all put in their time to work-out and train for the race. I am sure they all had coaches, trainers, etc. Why did not all of them end up with a prize? What made the difference?

It is true that they all ran the race, but only one of them got the prize— here's why.

Temperate in all Things.

Now, the Scripture in Corinthians 9:25 says that many compete for the prize. Only those who are *temperate in all things*, seem to have the edge in winning the race.

The word *temperate* in Greek means, *the power or lordship which one has either over oneself or over something.* To walk, run, or race in a *temperate mode* means that you have self-control over your own life. You don't allow your lower nature to dictate your moods (attitude) form of thinking, or your actions. Being temperate means that you control your life very well, both under peaceful or adverse conditions.

The Apostle Paul also reveals to us his perspective on what it means to take dominion over himself: Here's some of Paul's secrets...

•**Run, not with uncertainty:** Paul ran his race knowing where he was going, and knowing what he was doing. The Apostle Paul was not an individual without a road map. He knew exactly what he needed to do, and when.

•**Fight, not beating the air:** Here's an interesting picture: Paul fought with his fists, like a boxer. He knew exactly what it was that he was hitting, not just throwing punches at the air.

•**Discipline the body:.** Lastly, Paul reveals the secret by saying, *I discipline my body...* The word *discipline* here means to *strike under the eye.* In essence Paul was saying, *I punch my flesh into dominion — to the point that if I have to give it a black eye, I will do it – for the benefit of keeping my flesh in check.*

I believe this attitude exemplified by the Apostle Paul, is truly the key to any form of advancement in the kingdom. Discipline is truly the method of getting your body in shape and in motion for God!

Neh'enah.

16

The Author!

"Therefore we also, since we are surrounded by so great a cloud of witnesses, let us lay aside every weight, and the sin which so easily ensnares us, and let *us* run with endurance the race that is set before us, looking unto Jesus, the author and finisher of our faith, who for the joy that was set before Him endured the cross, despising the shame, and has sat down at the right hand of the throne of God." (Hebrews 12:1, 2)

Have you ever read a good romance novel? Or how about a book on someone's life? An autobiography? One thing is for certain, every chapter is made to keep us engaged with rich content.

In romance novels, you will find a love story filled with romance, intrigue, pain, and sorrow. Perhaps an important character may die, and if we are fortunate, we might see somebody piece their lives back together again!

All these elements are found in a good novel or biography. Great authors are experts in keeping their readers engaged with rich tone and mastery of words — so much so, that one chapter does not reveal the end of the story. You must keep reading every chapter to see the beauty of the whole story.

Jesus Is the Author of Our Lives!

In Hebrews 12:1, 2, the writer suggests or commands every believer to **"run with endurance the race that is set before us, looking unto Jesus, the author and finisher of *our* faith."**

The writer in Hebrews says that Jesus is the Author of our lives. Anything to do with our walk of faith, is written by Jesus, the author! He instituted this walk and thus leads us by His Spirit and writes our story as we follow Him.

We Might Miss Something of Value!

Returning to the illustration of reading novels or biographies— it would almost be a sin to stop halfway through reading a good book. Not a sin but almost one!

You see, if we stop reading halfway, we will miss out on a possible comeback. We might miss out on the tears and pain that is so much needed to appreciate a breakthrough in life.

If we *stick it out* and complete the full reading, we will appreciate the Author's gift in putting a story together. Let me just say that it is the same way in our personal lives with God as Author.

Just because we are going through a *rough patch* or a lonely desert in our lives doesn't mean that the Author is finished with the book. As a matter of fact, a good story will have many chapters that include tears, pain, and sorrow. We must learn to appreciate the Author — who will bring us through all the pain into a beautiful and glorious finish!

Our lives are no different.

A Little Drama Doesn't Hurt!

Jesus, the Author, is making a great story out of your life and mine. Your story and my story are still being written. Why be surprised when a negative chapter appears? We must know that it is only adding drama to a great finish!

The Lord is not done with you and me. He is still bringing us into fruition; He is still developing and cultivating maturity in us. Don't give up! Don't whine and complain! Don't turn your back on the Author! He is getting ready to write one of the greatest finishes ever to your life and mine!

Neh'enah.

17

Have You Been *Pushed Violently*?

> "You pushed me violently, that I might fall,
> But the Lord helped me.
> The Lord *is* my strength and song,
> And He has become my salvation." (Psalm 118:13, 14)

While meditating on this portion of Scripture, I learned of how wicked the enemy really is. I have always known about the devil and how vicious he can be, but in truth, he is not taking any prisoners; his sole intent is to kill the believer, not just trap him and embarrass him.

The Psalmist brings forth an interesting point to us in this Psalm 118:13, 14 and I quote: **"You pushed me violently, that I might fall…"**

It is the devil's intention to destroy us who are propagating the resurrection power of Jesus. If you propagate the message of the kingdom, he will come after you to silence you. As a matter of fact, all hell will rise against you to silence you. Be mindful of this!

When We Fall!

You must know this: It is the enemy's true joy to see us

lost and confused, to see us down and out, to make us believe that there is no hope for us. He will take our failures and multiply them in the presence of God and make fun of us. He will call us out in the presence of God and embarrass us as ultimate losers!

The enemy always pushes violently. He doesn't trip us, he doesn't tap us, he doesn't play tricks on us— the enemy pushes us, violently! It is all done with the intent to make us fall and hopefully never get up again!

Why Does the Enemy Fight with Such Intensity?

I believe the enemy fights with so much intensity because he knows he only has a small window of time. He keeps attacking and attacking with intention because he knows his future is coming to an end.

Listen to Revelation 12:12 says, **"Woe to the inhabitants of the earth and the sea! For the devil has come down to you, having great wrath, because he knows that he has a short time."**

It would be wise for us who serve the living God to be conscious of this enemy's tactics and strategies as he makes every effort and attempt to completely destroy us.

Learn to Navigate through the Attacks!

We must learn to navigate through the opposition. When tempted, we must know that God has prepared a door for us to escape. We will always have options: We can stand there and wonder what is happening, or we can run away from temptation.

The biggest mistake one can make is to be wise in their own eyes! To think that one can outsmart the enemy through their own wisdom and ability is a grave mistake. It has been proven in times past that we cannot defeat the flesh by using the flesh!

When tempted to attack someone who has offended us, betrayed us, maligned us, or hurt us in some way, don't pay them back the same way! Let us move in the opposite spirit and bless them instead. Let God take care of the *vengeance* part.

It is stuff like this that the enemy wants us to fail in. He knows we are upset, and he figures that we will want revenge — don't do it! Let us put our whole trust in the Lord; He can make us stand!

Neh'enah.

18

Equipped for this Strange Land!

> "Open my eyes, that I may see
> Wondrous things from Your law.
> I *am* a stranger in the earth;
> Do not hide Your commandments from me.
> My soul breaks with longing
> For Your judgments at all times." (Psalm 119:18-20)

It is clear to me that the Psalmist understood that there was more to reading the law for the sake of just reading it. Apparently, this man found instruction, vision, and guidance for the different areas of his life. When one is pleading with God, **"Open my eyes, that I may see wondrous things from Your law,"** you know that this individual is anxious and passionate about knowing what is next in their life.

I do believe that this philosophy of thinking can only breed success and daily satisfaction to anyone who practices it.

Let's go deeper in this very thought...

Strangers in the Earth

The Scripture says that the Psalmist is longing for his eyes to be open so that he might see what God is saying in His word. Why the anxious cry? Well, for starters, he says that he is a *stranger in the earth.* In other words, the Psalmist in essence is saying, *I don't belong to this world; I need heavenly guidance. I need you God to show me what you are thinking and how you see my life and the life around me."*

Is this our humble cry? Do we share the same motivation? Are we longing to see God's word clearer so that we may act on it, or do we just want to accumulate more knowledge?

The Psalmist called himself a *stranger.* In the original Hebrew text, this word means *foreigner.* We are foreigners in this world— we don't live by these standards but by God's Holy principles. *[see 1 Peter 2:11-12]*

We must get to the place where we are convinced that God's word is the road map to our destiny. Without God's leadership principles, we might end up in a ditch somewhere. We must ask God to help us grow in this desire!

Breaking with Longing for More!

**"My soul breaks with longing
For Your judgments at all times."**

You would think that the Psalmist is exaggerating with his desire for more but let me just say that there is a time when

God will touch you so powerfully that your whole being will be consumed with this fiery passion.

"My soul breaks with longing," in its original language means, *my inner self is broken with desire for more!*

Have you ever felt such a strong burning for more of Jesus? Have you been to the place where if He didn't speak to you through His word, you would die? If you haven't been there, you must get there!

In closing, I know that the world has its own voices calling out your name. Its intent is to occupy you with nothing but vain ideas and philosophies. Just like your flesh longs to be fed garbage, and yearns to be filled with earthly filth — so the Spirit of the Lord within you, hungers, and thirst for holiness. Who will you feed?

Neh'enah.

19

Continuous Weeping!

**"Those who sow in tears
Shall reap in joy.
He who continually goes forth weeping,
Bearing seed for sowing,
Shall doubtless come again with rejoicing,
Bringing his sheaves *with him*."** (Psalm 126:5, 6)

There is something to be said of someone who constantly yearns for God's will to be done in them— for God's purposes to be accomplished in some way during their lifetime.

Please note: This attitude and mindset is not normal. This is not the cry of the 97% in the Christian church today!

Most believers are wrapped up in *self*. It's what they want, it's what they need, and will press in like a stubborn child until they get their way. My friends, this is not God's way!

Sowing in Tears!

When I read these verses, my spirit is stirred within. Two things come to my mind: the first one is the word *sowing*, and the second word is *tears*.

Reaping in Joy!

The reward of sowing will eventually come. When? We don't know. All we know is that if we sow into the earth, eventually, the mercy of God will come and produce fruit for our eyes to behold. Joy will flood our hearts when this happens.

My friends, this is the principle of sowing and reaping. This might be a one-time event in our lives, but wait, there is so much more. It can become a lifestyle. You see, for the immature, a one-time experience can take place and they are happy with the results, but for those who want to make this a lifestyle, they must continually do it.

He Who continually Goes Forth Weeping...

Let me just say right here that there is another group of people who believe in this principle; they are those who practice this daily. It is not a one-time event with them. They have discovered the secret of reaping, and they will not stop sowing in tears! Are you one of these people?

Understanding the Process

To understand the law of sowing and reaping, one must first learn the process. Now, the process of sowing is not very difficult— the true test begins to unfold when one must cultivate what has been planted, water the seed, dig around it, and wait! Three days later, you get to do it all over again. This is God's way!

You don't reap anything until you have lived out the process. To receive anything before hand, before maturity arrives, is only to fool yourself. Many don't want to grow a garden because it demands time, effort, money, patience, and hard work. Nothing will measure your success until you have seen something grow.

The curse of this age is that we want everything *now*! We are so used to having everything given to us at our immediate request. The microwave oven is even slow for some people. God forbid that your popcorn takes 15 seconds longer to cook than normal. You would probably be calling the company that made the microwave and demand your money back! (I'm exaggerating, but just a little!)

Learn to sow in tears, so that you may reap in joy. This has been God's way from the beginning of time, and it will continue to be God's way till the end of time! It would be wise to learn God's ways as we journey through this life. It will be worth it all!

Neh'enah.

20

The Full Counsel of God

"For I have not shunned to declare to you the whole counsel of God. Therefore take heed to yourselves and to all the flock, among which the Holy Spirit has made you overseers, to shepherd the church of God which He purchased with His own blood. For I know this, that after my departure savage wolves will come in among you, not sparing the flock. Also, from among yourselves men will rise up, speaking perverse things, to draw away the disciples after themselves. Therefore watch, and remember that for three years I did not cease to warn everyone night and day with tears." (Acts 20:27-31)

Last night while I slept, I had this dream. Let me share with you...

The dream begins when an old friend was down visiting family and it happened that we bumped into each other. I'm not very clear where we met, but we exchanged a few pleasantries.

The scene changed, and now I was preaching at a church somewhere and he happened to be in the service. He sat and heard the message. When the service was over, he approached me and said, "You are still preaching those holiness messages?"

I said, "Is there anything else we are called to preach?" (I made this remark with a sarcastic comment.) He then proceeded to rebuke me for preaching such a strong message full of prophetic content and said, "Those messages are so irrelevant with the times! No one will come and hear you. You need to preach messages that are more soothing and not so direct and convictive! People are hurting and they need a message to make them feel good!"

I remember listening and seeing my friend's expression towards me — his expression had changed towards me. The dream ended.

When I woke up this morning after having that dream, I was a bit troubled. I went to the Lord and said to Him, *Maybe my friend was right. What right do I have to preach that way? After all, I am probably the least likely of all people to be preaching these kinds of messages?*

To this the Lord replied and said to me, *David, I called you to preach the whole counsel of God, not what tickles people's ears and makes them feel good!*

This Pampered Age!

This devotion today expresses my heartfelt burden for the lack of God's whole counsel being spoken at the local churches.

Many pastors today have bowed to the god of this age. They have begun to *market* their ministries with the goal to give people what people want, and not what God demands. The gospel of Christ has been watered down to the place where the gospel of the kingdom has become one of many ideas for spiritual vitality, not the single idea that is in God's heart!

There is no more seeking of God first, **"then all these things will be added unto you!"** [see Matthew 6:33]

In this pampered age where interest is in popularity, crowds, and finances, we have moved away from God's agenda. I know the times are trying and very difficult—along with political differences, riots, and the pandemic, and because of finances, ministries are at the verge of shutting down! I get it.

Despite all that is happening in our drunken world, we are called to be faithful to the cause of Christ. We are responsible as ministers of a new covenant to preach the whole counsel of God!

The Order

Called to Love Him (this is inward): God has called us to lead others into falling in love with Jesus with all their heart, not just part of it. To give God a full-hearted devotion with both mind and heart.

Called to Walk with Him *(this is outward)*: Out of our personal experience and intimacy with God, we are called to walk out what we have seen and heard. This is our ministry that we take into the streets. Intimacy with God will prompt us to go out and touch someone with the gospel of the kingdom.

Called to Serve Him *(this is external)*: Expressing Jesus to the world is one of our responsibilities. We must be about the Father's business daily, not only when it's convenient. When people see us, they must see Christ!

Called to Be like Him *(this is eternal)*: Allowing the Holy Spirit to have His way in us is the first step into transformation. If we give the Spirit permission to change us, He will. Remember, He is not like us. He will have to break old molds, traditions, and mindsets, to get us to the place God needs us to be!

I trust that the God of peace will enlighten us to walk out His full counsel and that He won't stop until we are conformed to His image. No matter what comes our way to deter us!

Neh'enah.

21

God's Real Pleasure!

**"He does not delight in the strength of the horse;
He takes no pleasure in the legs of a man.
The Lord takes pleasure in those who fear Him,
In those who hope in His mercy."** (Psalm 147:10, 11)

All through Scripture, we see this same idea being spoken or prophesied about at different times in the history of Israel, the ministry of Jesus, and the early church. What idea am I referring to? I'm referring to the idea that people should not put their trust in human strength, wisdom, or ability!

There is a reason why God is bringing this verse to light today. It might be that you are one of those servants of God who has lost their way by putting your whole confidence in humanity alone. Perhaps now you are making your way back to the straight and narrow path. Then again, you might be the person who today is trying to make a decision that will get you from point A to point B, and at the same time, glorify God through it all!

Whatever the situation is in your own life today, God will always honor and help **"those who fear Him."**

Maybe it's just me, but this I have seen — that those who **"hope in His mercy,"** seem to always get the greatest portion!

The Scripture plainly reads,
"The Lord takes pleasure in those who fear Him!"

When we can get a better understanding that we are here because of God's mercy and His goodwill toward mankind, then we can better understand our position. He is the Leader— we are the followers. He is our Shepherd, and we are the sheep of His pasture!

But Because God Loves You!

It's safe to say that it wasn't the fame or glory that God saw in us when he took us in. It was not that at all. Let's look at it:

"For you *are* a holy people to the Lord your God; the Lord your God has chosen you to be a people for Himself, a special treasure above all the peoples on the face of the earth. The Lord did not set His love on you nor choose you because you were more in number than any other people, for you were the least of all peoples; but because the Lord loves you, and because He would keep the oath which He swore to your fathers, the Lord has brought you out with a mighty hand, and redeemed you from the house of bondage, from the hand of Pharaoh

king of Egypt." (Deuteronomy 7:6-8)

There is nothing that we could have done to make God like us or love us — but His love and mercy caught a glimpse of our weakness and frailty. He saw that we **"were the least of all peoples,"** and without a second thought, He reached out and loved us!

To God forever be the glory for setting His eyes upon us!

When we acknowledge God in our midst and know that He longs to be engaged with us in our decision-making, He will take pleasure in us. I do believe that when we live this way, this puts a huge smile on His face! Thank you, Jesus, for touching my life!

Neh'enah.

22

The Need for Diligence!

**"Keep your heart with all diligence,
For out of it *spring* the issues of life."** (Proverbs 4:23)

As I meditated upon these few verses, I came to this powerful word from the writings of Solomon.

I must ask myself the question, *Is there anything more valuable in life than to keep guard against self?* I think not! To keep oneself must be the priority for all of us. Keeping guard over our heart, emotions, mind, actions, and deeds —must be placed at the highest place on our agenda. To not be proactive about this can be detrimental to our destiny!

First, let me say that the word *keep* in Hebrew means, to watch or keep guard. Picture a soldier keeping watch over an assigned area. They must be disciplined enough to not move or leave their post. It is the same description King Solomon is giving us regarding our heart. Our *heart* speaks of our inner being (the spirit-being) where God lives!

Not only are we to keep our hearts nonchalantly, but we are asked to keep it with all diligence. What does diligence mean here? Well, I studied this specific word and found out that in its original language, *diligence* means, *a place of confinement, jail, prison, guard, watch, observance.*

In short, we are called to keep our hearts and protect them as if we were keeping watch over a prison. Do you see this? What comes in and what comes out, must be observed and watched intentionally. We can't afford to be negligent or careless with our thought patterns, our emotions, or with words we speak or actions we take. We must be more accountable with our hearts!

What We Put In!

Living here on earth is a challenge for any American. Bombarded with countless ideas and philosophies, we are always challenged to do what is right. Now, many things are not of our preference, but they may be God's preference!

Our flesh has a different idea of what it means to serve God. The flesh looks for anything that pleases self and causes division with God. The flesh is our lower nature; it won't please God because it can't! It will always challenge the will of God.

Feed on the Lord's will. Read the word of God and learn what's expected from someone who lives in the kingdom of God. Be a student of the Bible!

What We Keep Out!

As we do our best to follow the Spirit of God, the flesh will continue to challenge our conscience. It will do everything in its arsenal to keep us away from pleasing Him who created us. This is the work of the flesh.

Thoughts that make you feel less, thoughts of failure, negative thoughts that bring your emotions low— all these must be checked in at the door. Negative people who surround you might have to go!

The Issues of Life

Remember why you started guarding your heart at first! It was with the intent to have a better path for your life. The Lord knows that whatever is allowed to remain in you, whether good or bad, will eventually spring out.

If the thoughts that you harbor are good, then you will be a blessing to God, to yourself and to others. If the thoughts you are allowing to come in are negative in nature, and you deliberately cling to them— you will only hurt yourself and others.

With all your strength, keep guard with all diligence!

Neh'enah.

23

The Immeasurable-ness of God!   Part 1.

Light Out of Darkness!

"For it is the God who commanded light to shine out of darkness, who has shone in our hearts to *give* the light of the knowledge of the glory of God in the face of Jesus Christ." (2 Corinthians 4:6)

"In the beginning God created the heavens and the earth. The earth was without form, and void; and darkness *was* on the face of the deep. And the Spirit of God was hovering over the face of the waters. Then God said, 'Let there be light'; and there was light." (Genesis 1:1-3)

The immeasurable-ness of God has to do with God's mercy upon our lives. Things are not always given to us because we deserve them. Sometimes, things are just given *purely* through God's mercy and grace!

We must learn to see God in this light. It is really and truly not about us, but instead about His great mercy!

The Carnal Mind

I have come to know in my own experience with God that

the carnal mind and the natural mind, do not appreciate the spiritual mind. It doesn't want to hear God's thoughts and much less obey them. As a matter of fact, the carnal mind is the enemy of God!

It goes something like this:

If God offers healing; the carnal mind says, *Impossible!* If the Spirit of God speaks of restoration; the carnal mind says, *It will never happen!* If the mind of the Lord says, *It can still be salvaged*, the carnal mind says, *It's too late!*

Listen to this story:

"After this there was a feast of the Jews, and Jesus went up to Jerusalem. Now there is in Jerusalem by the Sheep *Gate* **a pool, which is called in Hebrew, Bethesda, having five porches. In these lay a great multitude of sick people, blind, lame, paralyzed, waiting for the moving of the water. For an angel went down at a certain time into the pool and stirred up the water; then whoever stepped in first, after the stirring of the water, was made well of whatever disease he had. Now a certain man was there who had an infirmity thirty-eight years. When Jesus saw him lying there, and knew that he already had been** *in that condition* **a long time, He said to him, 'Do you want to be made well?'**

The sick man answered Him, 'Sir, I have no man to put

me into the pool when the water is stirred up; but while I am coming, another steps down before me.'

Jesus said to him, 'Rise, take up your bed and walk.'

And immediately the man was made well, took up his bed, and walked." (John 5:1-9)

Are you familiar with this story?

The sick man who had been there by the waters, had been sick for thirty-eight years; perhaps he thought that this was the way life would be and end-up!

When Jesus appeared to him, he asked, **"Do you want to be made well?"**

The sick man didn't say yes or no, he just explained why things had not been working out for him. He gives a full explanation to Jesus, listen: **"The sick man answered Him, 'Sir, I have no man to put me into the pool when the water is stirred up; but while I am coming, another steps down before me.'"**

Naturally, the man can't be blamed for not trying! He was honest and just simply saw no way out. Have you been in this same place? I know we all have been at our own crossroads.

In thinking that God's awesome power is contingent upon our emotions or our own faith, we err exceedingly! We look at the natural circumstance and conclude— this will not work!

God is not limited or bound by what we see, hear, or feel. He will breakthrough despite the impossibility.

It Has Nothing to Do with How I Feel!

One of the things I have learned as I follow Christ is that His mercy endures forever. His mercy is not contingent upon my emotions or my intellect. He is not waiting for me to get it together— He knows that I am nothing but dust!

I believe that this is the reason that when we are faced with a *giant* in our lives, one that we can't handle in our own strength— He immediately steps in!

Just when we think that something is over and done, impossible, or overwhelming, the Lord always surprises us with something altogether different. Very different from our thinking and very different from our expectations!

For example…

Light Out of Darkness!

When I think of God's immeasurableness, I also think of faith— God's faith.

Unless we have developed a life of faith, we will not be able to comprehend God's immeasurableness! It is impossible to capture a life filled with signs and wonders if we don't have the faith of God.

What always seems to be impossible with people— it is not impossible with God. Our mind only reaches to a certain point and then it fades; God's mind moves in a totally different light. When God acts, He does it in such a way that it leaves us in awe and wondering how it was possible to do it.

Have you ever been in a very dark and difficult situation? Maybe it wasn't this dramatic, but it was nevertheless difficult. You wondered and wondered how you were going to get out of something.. You did the math, you received the counsel, you made the arrangements, but in the end, nothing got fixed. Then, when it seemed to be out of your reach, light came forth *out of darkness*!

This is exactly what the immeasurableness of God is. He is not limited to my thinking and experience. He doesn't march to my drum beat! He has His own.

Chaos Invites His Spirit!

Look at this: In the beginning, the Scripture says, *the world was void, without form and dark.* This looks like a lot of chaos to me.

What is man to do with such a calamity? Man, probably panics and leaves it alone; others, run from the calamity, yet others wait upon the Lord to do the *impossible*!

Has your heart ever caught a glimpse of what God can do with chaos? Have you been taken to this dimension, where *light comes out of darkness*? If you haven't been to this place, eventually you will.

As I close my meditation today, I need you to be on the lookout for *light coming out of darkness* in your own life. If your life is peachy and perfect right now, I am happy for you. Take this message and put it in your back pocket; save it for a rainy day.

The lesson for today is: look for light to come out of darkness. Don't make an impulsive and extreme move until God has had a chance to demonstrate His power!

Neh'enah.

24

The Immeasurable-ness of God!   Part 2

Calling Out Those Things Which Do Not Exist as Though They Did!

"Abraham, who is the father of us all (as it is written, *I have made you a father of many nations*) in the presence of Him whom he believed—God, who gives life to the dead and calls those things which do not exist as though they did...". (Romans 4:16, 17)

Pondering early this morning about God's immeasurable-ness, I came across another biblical truth— calling out ***"those things which do not exist as though they did!"***

Wow! What an amazing thought!   In our carnal intellectual mind, it is impossible to see it, yet in the Spirit of God, all things are possible!

Let me begin by making this one statement: *From where God stands, there are no limitations whatsoever!*

God doesn't look at night and day and considers them as a hindrance; He doesn't look at mountains to cross as obstacles; He simply flies over them! He doesn't look at *giants* as tall human beings that are powerful and scary; He still crushes them and takes their heads off by His mighty power!

God Can See for Miles!

One of the things we must diligently turn our attention to is the fact that God always knows what He is about to do. He is always *miles* ahead of everyone else. He sees the past, the present, and the future.

Let us look at this testimony:

"Now the Passover, a feast of the Jews, was near. Then Jesus lifted up *His* eyes, and seeing a great multitude coming toward Him, He said to Philip, 'Where shall we buy bread, that these may eat?'

But this He said to test him, for He Himself knew what He would do." (John 6:4-6)

Jesus saw the multitudes coming way before they started arriving; Jesus saw the need to feed them long before they even knew they would be hungry. Yes, Jesus did *pick on* Philip, by posing the question, **"Where shall we buy bread that these may eat?"**

After the question is made to Philip, John the writer tells us about the intent behind the question: *"...this He said to test him, for He Himself knew what He would do."*

The Lord knows things way before they materialize; He sees into the future, and then decides if He wants to invite us to participate in shaping it!

Let us look at this other testimony:

"Now Jericho was securely shut up because of the children of Israel; none went out, and none came in. And the Lord said to Joshua: 'See! I have given Jericho into your hand, its king, *and* the mighty men of valor. You shall march around the city, all *you* men of war; you shall go all around the city once. This you shall do six days. And seven priests shall bear seven trumpets of rams' horns before the ark. But the seventh day you shall march around the city seven times, and the priests shall blow the trumpets. It shall come to pass, when they make a long *blast* with the ram's horn, *and* when you hear the sound of the trumpet, that all the people shall shout with a great shout; then the wall of the city will fall down flat. And the people shall go up every man straight before him.'" (Joshua 6:1-5)

When God told Joshua to march around the walls of Jericho, He knew exactly what He was going to do to those impenetrable walls. He simply wanted man to cooperate by doing what he could with his natural strength; it was God who would do His part (the supernatural) in response to man's obedience!

As you can read in the book of Joshua chapter 6, the mission was accomplished!

It is obvious that God doesn't think, process, or worry like we do. In God's economy — He rules the whole earth! Everything is naked before Him, and all things are subject to Him; yes, all things were created by Him and for Him!

Abraham, the Father of Us All!

Now, let us look at how God's immeasurableness affects our daily lives. The Scripture in Romans 4 shows us Father Abraham, our father of faith. He pretty much laid out the pattern of how we should walk with God. He moved from one faith event to another— this was his lifestyle.

In church, this is our lifestyle as well, if we accept to follow God by faith!

Now, Abraham was made a promise by God Himself when He was more or less, 75 years of age. He was told that his wife Sarah would have a son. Well, that son had not yet come and now they were nearing 100 hundred years of age. God made a promise and 25 years had already passed with no child!

Was God joking when He made that promise to them? Was the Lord too busy to attend to that promise? Or did God *simply* forget? So many thoughts fill our hearts when things seem to get a bit out of control. Not knowing what comes next, puts many of us on a tailspin— doesn't it?

Yet, throughout all of this wondering, God had it all under His control. God was not worried about how man looks at life, at challenges, at impossibilities! When God gets ready to act, He acts and gets the desired results —all the time!

You see, in God's mind, everything He says, it already exists. Our eyes might not be able to see all that God is doing, but that is irrelevant. Therefore, the Scripture reads, "(He) **calls those things which do not exist as though they did!"**

Everything God speaks, already exists by the power of His word! Every promise that God makes can be taken to the bank! It will manifest in God's timing!

Neh'enah.

25

The Immeasurable-ness of God!   Part 3.

What Do You Have?

"So, Elisha said to her, 'What shall I do for you? Tell me, what do you have in the house?'

And she said, 'Your maidservant has nothing in the house but a jar of oil.'" (2 Kings 4:2)

"One of His disciples, Andrew, Simon Peter's brother, said to Him, 'There is a lad here who has five barley loaves and two small fish, but what are they among so many?'" (John 6:8, 9)

Once again, we see the immeasurableness of God in these passages. What seems to be impossible for man is never impossible with God! I am always amazed at how God makes things happen and repeatedly proves Himself faithful.

Let's begin with the situation that the widow had at hand. She needed a miracle and had no clue where this miracle would come from. Her husband, who had just died, was in debt and the collectors needed payment to be made. There was no way this widow could make the payment, so the collectors would be taking away her sons as slaves to pay her debt.

This was a very stressful situation for this widow and as if it wasn't enough to have lost her husband, the thought of losing her children was certainly unbearable. It was during this experience that she cried out to the prophet of God, Elisha.

When you don't have anything to fix your situation, and you can't find any comfort in your surroundings, what do you do next? You call upon the immeasurable God!

The Lord may come and ask you, *What do you have in your house?* It almost seems like God is looking for anything of substance, so that He may perform His magic! When you offer the little you have, He will take it and multiply it! It seems like God is always looking for an excuse to multiply His mighty power!

Are You Sure There is Nothing More?

As I studied and prayed, I came to the realization that when God is asking the widow that one deep question, *What do you have in your house?* What the Lord (through the Prophet Elisha) is really saying or at least attempting to convey to this widow is, *Are you positive that there is nothing in your house? I mean, have you exhausted all means of saving yourself? Are you sure that you can't save yourself and you need me to perform a miracle?*

I believe that in response to her honest answer of saying, **"Your maidservant has nothing in the house but a jar of oil."**

God knew she wasn't lying, and the Lord was able to act mightily on her behalf!

When the woman surrendered the little jar of oil and placed it in God's hands, God ran with it! This widow never looked back.

An Early Wake-Up Call!

I have personally been through some experiences where I had nothing to work with, and God showed up and proved Himself strong on my behalf.

During the early years of my ministry, I had an early wake-up call in the realm of faith. Financial issues were always knocking at my door. Unable to pay bills, rent, buy curriculum, and make ends meet at home, was always putting pressure on me. Holiday seasons were very challenging times for my wife and me. In all this, God showed Himself faithful and always enabled us to keep going forward without getting bitter and discouraged.

When God is getting ready to move in our lives, He trains

us in the gift of faith. There are no guarantees but God. That is all we need!

What Are They Among So Many?

In the same sense, when the Lord Jesus wanted to feed the multitude, He asked one of His disciples to help.. The disciples were puzzled and wondered how on God's green earth this was going to happen.

Have you ever been in a place where the need was great, and the resources were few? Have you ever been faced with an impossibility and just folded your hands in despair? I am almost positive that you have!

This was the same case at hand. The disciple simply said, "There is a lad here who has five barley loaves and two small fish, but what are they among so many?"

What a great observation; what a great question! Again, here we see more questions than answers.

It was the Lord who lives in a different dimension who made the miracle happen. He took what was available, prayed and multiplied it! Listen to this: **"And Jesus took the loaves, and when He had given thanks He distributed *them* to the disciples, and the disciples to those sitting down; and likewise of the fish, as much as they wanted. So, when they were filled, He said to His disciples,**

'Gather up the fragments that remain, so that nothing is lost.'" (John 6:11, 12)

It's not how much you have on hand that God uses — it's the faith you have in your heart that makes all the difference!

Neh'enah.

26

The Immeasurable-ness of God!   Part 4.

Have You Ever Laughed at God?

"Then they said to him, 'Where is Sarah your wife?'

So, he said, 'Here, in the tent.'

And He said, 'I will certainly return to you according to the time of life, and behold, Sarah your wife shall have a son.'

Sarah was listening in the tent door which was behind him. Now Abraham and Sarah were old, well advanced in age; and Sarah had passed the age of childbearing. Therefore, Sarah laughed within herself, saying, 'After I have grown old, shall I have pleasure, my lord being old also?'" (Genesis 18:9-12)

I have found some golden nuggets to share with you, and I want to unfold this truth carefully and share my heart with you.

Recognizing God!

"Then the Lord appeared to him by the terebinth trees

of Mamre, as he was sitting in the tent door in the heat of the day. So he lifted his eyes and looked, and behold, three men were standing by him; and when he saw *them*, he ran from the tent door to meet them, and bowed himself to the ground..." (Genesis 18:1, 2)

It was another regular day in the life of Abraham— nothing was different than the previous day. Same situation, same prayer burdens, still contending for the promise that Jehovah God had given him 25 years ago but becoming dimmer and dimmer as the days, weeks, months, and years, passed.

The promise that he would have a son was becoming more and more of a joke than an actual reality. The idea that he and his wife Sarah would have children was now impossible, and like most of us, they simply left it in the Lord's hands.

But it was on this day that something was about to change...

The Scripture says that God showed up in three persons (sounds like the whole trinity showed up for this one)!

As Abraham saw what was unfolding before him, the word of God says, **"and when he saw *them*, he ran from the tent door to meet them..."**

He ran with certainty that it was God coming to visit them! He didn't wonder if it was God, he didn't call his wife to come and see, he didn't slowly make his way out of the tent….NO SIR! What did he do? The Scripture says, **"he ran from the tent door to meet them."**

It is obvious to me that a man or woman of God who has unfinished business with God will not sit idle waiting for something to happen. They will be pacing back and forth in prayer with a heart full of expectation; yes, they will be waiting with anticipation of what is to come!

Let your heart now ponder this: Are you waiting for God to come through for you? Get ready to run towards Him! He is coming and His reward is with Him! Amen.

Running Towards Him!

When your spirit is awakened to the reality of His presence, you will begin to live a life full of expectation. You will march to the beat of a different drummer. While everyone is following the herd of people going one way, you will be going the opposite to where the real presence of Jesus is!

Abraham ran towards the presence of the Lord! When the Lord is King of our life, and He holds that authority over us— we will see Jesus in everything!

Some Stayed Behind!

At the scent of the presence of God, you would think that Sarah would also have run towards God, but she did not! She stayed in the tent. Why did she stay in? Obviously, Sarah had a different take on all this: She might have been so disillusioned for years due to the unfulfilled promise or she might just have been sick of all this revival rhetoric, and she didn't want to see it or hear about it anymore. Whatever her reasoning, Sarah stayed in.

I think that too often we make the attempt to equate ourselves with God. We think that God thinks like us, He processes like us, and that He sympathizes with our carnal reasoning. Here's what I have found out about this: God is altogether different than me!

Laughing at Impossibilities

Now, here's an interesting exchange that took place as these three men visited Abraham. Listen to this:

"Then they said to him, 'Where is Sarah your wife?'
So he said, 'Here, in the tent.'
And He said, 'I will certainly return to you according to the time of life, and behold, Sarah your wife shall have a son.' (Sarah was listening in the tent door which *was* behind him.)

Now Abraham and Sarah were old, well advanced in age; and Sarah had passed the age of childbearing. Therefore, Sarah laughed within herself, saying, 'After I have grown old, shall I have pleasure, my lord being old also?'" (Genesis 18:9-12)

Here's the result of hiding in tents, instead of recognizing the presence of God and running towards it. Abraham ran towards God, and Sarah stayed in the tent. Is it any wonder why we laugh at impossibilities? It's hard to doubt God when He is standing right in front of us!

The tent is a symbol of hiding; it's a house of fear and doubt and unbelief. Staying in a tent has a way of disengaging us from His presence. As a matter of fact, the word **tent** in Hebrew means a *home*. Can you see this? A *home* carries a connotation of settling. Settled and no need to press in into anything. Sarah should have known that she wasn't home yet. There were many things, yet that God had prepared for her and her husband.

As I close this word, the immeasurableness of God doesn't look at impossibilities (which are man-made thoughts). He looks at all things created as opportunities to reveal Himself in greater ways for His good pleasure!

Neh'enah.

27

The Immeasurable-ness of God! Part 5.

Do Not Consider Your Own Body!

"And not being weak in faith, he did not consider his own body, already dead (since he was about a hundred years old), and the deadness of Sarah's womb." (Romans 4:19)

In meditating upon this theme on the immeasurable-ness of God, I have come to understand more and more — that unless the faith of God is activated in our lives, we won't be able to see, feel, touch, sense, or experience the immeasurable-ness of God. Of this, I am positive!

The Scripture in Hebrews 11:6 that reads, **"But without faith it is impossible to please *Him*, for he who comes to God must believe that He is, and *that* He is a rewarder of those who diligently seek Him."**

This is fundamental for all who desire to walk in the supernatural power of Christ. Is it any wonder why so few engage in this lifestyle of signs and wonders, not to mention miracles?

The Ability to Know!

It's one thing to understand this verse in Hebrews 11:6, but altogether something different to live it and walk it out daily. As a matter of fact, I don't believe you can have an impact on anyone, including your own world, without the supernatural power of God operating in you and through you!

When I think of active faith or the faith of God, I think of a supernatural impartation of confidence that what was said, declared, transferred, or downloaded into our human spirit, will happen just as it was told! This is the kind of faith that moves mountains, yes, it is the kind of faith that *pleases* God. When you know that you know!

Abraham's Confidence!

Abraham's confidence in what God told him 25 years earlier was still as fresh as when God prophesied over him the promised son, Isaac. I think at times, he might have wondered what had happened to the promise, but nevertheless, Abraham still *believed in God!*

Abraham did not need to *psyche* himself into believing; he didn't have the need to confess anything of what God had spoken to him, and Abraham didn't go around decreeing anything in the name of the Lord. Abraham simply believed God. He held on to what God told him *personally*, and with full assurance, Abraham knew that a promise was still on its way— regardless of the circumstances!

It's What God Said!

When it came down to dealing with the opposing thoughts of doubt, fear, uncertainty, and insecurity, Abraham didn't flinch. He didn't look to the left or to the right— no sir, He looked into the face of Jehovah God and told him, *You said! You told me a son was on its way!* Oh, what a tiny ounce of faith in God that Abraham had!

When the three men showed up at Abraham's tent, and his wife Sarah was in the tent, one of the men prophesied to Abraham and told him that the following year he and his wife would have a son. Remember, this made Sarah laugh, yet, God was on schedule for a glorious miracle to take place.

He did NOT Consider His Own Body!

I believe that it was at this time that the book of Romans reveals the heart of Abraham as he heard the prophetic words uttered, that his heart and mind were altered; he then took on a different attitude and believed God, just listen: **"And not being weak in faith, he did not consider his own body, already dead (since he was about a hundred years old) and the deadness of Sarah's womb."**

Before I close this word, let me say that in our walk with God, we will have to be altered by the Spirit of the Lord and not simply just consider what we have at hand. We can either believe what people say, doctors say, professionals say, or we can believe what God told us— not considering our own limitations!

I believe that it is time to hear what God is saying to us and expect to see His glory at every circumstance. He is not limited one bit; He is the immeasurable God!

Neh'enah.

28

Baptized into Jesus!

"For as many of you as were baptized into Christ have put on Christ." (Galatians 3:27)

When speaking of spiritual revivals and awakenings, one must wonder how these events happen in a person's life. Does it just simply come upon you? Does someone impart this awakening into your life? Is there anything that a person can do to make this happen or prevent it from happening? Who does it come upon? Have you had the privilege of experiencing God at a whole different level in your personal life?

I have experienced impartations from God alone, and I have also received impartation from others as they laid their hands upon me that I may be touched by God. I do believe in impartation, and I believe also in personal visitations from the Lord. As a matter of fact, the Lord said that He would visit us and make His home in us! **"And he who loves Me will be loved by My Father, and I will love him and manifest Myself to him."**

Jesus also said, **"If anyone loves Me, he will keep My word; and My Father will love him, and We will come to him and make Our home with him."** (John 14:21-23)

As you read this portion of Scriptures, you know well that God has all the intentions of visiting our lives. What He does with us or in us when He comes is up to Him! All we can do is be attentive to His wishes and move when He tells us to.

What Is Baptism?

Now unto baptism— what is it? As I read Galatians 3:27, I kept meditating on its message repeatedly until it started to get a grip of my heart. When the Lord speaks of baptism, we tend to think of *water* baptism. In some places (churches, denominations, or religious groups) they still sprinkle people with water for baptism. In most Christian churches, water baptism is done by way of immersion. Immersion means *to put under*. This is a closer definition and action of what it means to be water-baptized according to the Scriptural pattern, at least in the book of Acts.

While reading this verse, I also set myself to do a word study on this very word. I did not think that the Apostle Paul was speaking of *water* baptism in this one verse in Galatians, so I had to dig deep for what exactly he was trying to convey.

Here's what I got:

For starters, the word *baptized* means to dip in or under. Another definition of the word *baptized* is *to dye*. As an example, *to dye material into another color*. The definition gets a little more interesting when you dig deeper. The word *baptized* also means to immerse and/or to sink the ship. It also means to go under.

What a varied set of definitions we find in this one word **baptized**— don't you agree?

As valuable and as defining as a water-baptism experience is, it still does not replace or substitute the idea of being baptized into Jesus! If you have been water-baptized already, good for you! If you have accepted Christ as Lord and Savior, then you should be water-baptized already. If you haven't yet, you need to decide and do it!

Now, if you have not accepted Christ as Savior and Lord, then all you did when you got water-baptized is get wet! That was all.

Have you Been Baptized into Jesus?

I want to take you into a real baptism with Jesus. I can't do it for you; it is all based on your faith and obedience to God.

How do I know if I have been baptized into Jesus? Just because one prays a prayer or repeats a sinner's prayer, or just because someone told you that by coming to church your life will change— that won't work! All that I have mentioned is not baptism into Jesus!

We just saw the definition of the word baptism or baptized:
- Have you *been dipped into or under Jesus*?

- Have you been *dyed* into Jesus, as to take a new color?

- Have you been *immersed* into Jesus as if you were *a ship that sank*?

- Have you gone under (your old self dying) into Christ Jesus?

One must realize it for themselves if they have taken on a new color, as if they had dyed themselves into Jesus. Unless this happens, following Jesus and pleasing the Father Heart of God, will be impossible!

Neh'enah.

29

Don't Fool Yourself!

"Brethren, if a man is overtaken in any trespass, you who *are* spiritual restore such a one in a spirit of gentleness, considering yourself lest you also be tempted. Bear one another's burdens, and so fulfill the law of Christ. For if anyone thinks himself to be something, when he is nothing, he deceives himself." (Galatians 6:1-3)

While I meditated on these few verses, my mind took me back to the many times that I had looked down upon the failures of others. It is perhaps the easiest thing to do when one thinks that they are better than someone else. What a trap has been laid out for humans— to think more highly of ourselves than we should!

Let me just add that thinking higher than oneself is not a self-esteem problem— it's a sin problem. It is that horrible thing that lurks every time someone applauds us or praises us for some achievement.

I am of the persuasion that there is nothing more foolish for a person than to think that they are better than someone else— but then one day walk up a path and find out that they're no different than the lowest of the low!

When a man realizes that he has been going down a wrong path and makes the necessary changes to get back on track, I believe that man should be brought in and restored in the gentleness of Christ. At least the Apostle Paul felt this way. I mean, what gain is there, if we lose a brother or a sister from God's army to the hands of the enemy?

I believe that believers have a real test to overcome when a fallen Christian fails, to restore them and not kick them when they are down! What an opportunity to manifest the gentleness of Christ!

Considering Yourself!

One of the challenges in restoring a fallen person, is that we who are spiritual, need to reach out considering ourselves, lest we also be tempted. Are you getting this? In other words, people who think that they are more spiritual, tend to stay away instead of reaching out. Why do they do this? My conclusion or at least one of them is that they are full of pride and to some degree arrogant! How do I know this? Because I have been there!

It's Time to Bear One Another's Burdens!

In reading God's word, we find so much wisdom and strength for our spiritual soul. We discover the heart and mind of God, and boy, do we need His counsel!

Because we tend to be selfish by nature, it often takes quite a bit to get ourselves out of our comfort zone and help someone else get through a dark night or season in their lives.

The Apostle Paul says, "Bear one another's burdens and so fulfill the law of Christ!"

I mean, for people like us who want to be like Jesus, we must learn this one principle— love the unlovable, reach out to the untouchable, care for the brokenhearted and pray for those in God's army in need of our prayers! May the Lord give us this heart!

The Hindrance!

What hinders people from going all out for someone else? I believe the hindrance to our expression of Christ is our selfish nature. We love ourselves way too much and we always want to be the ones *on top!*

When we see someone that we admire, we tend to criticize them. In some strange way, we feel that they are living the life we want and that there is not a single opportunity for us to have it— unless they fail, falter, disappear, and then we can take over! We would never admit to this, but I know that this is exactly what runs through the minds of the *selfish*. Oh yes, we don't say this to anybody, we only subconsciously wish it would happen!

Don't Deceive Yourself!

As I close this meditation, the Apostle Paul says something very deep here: **"For if anyone thinks himself to be something, when he is nothing, he deceives himself."**

Here's what I get from the Apostle Paul: When someone you know is overtaken by a trespass, we who are spiritual ought to help them during this time of testing. Now, the believer who hears about it, can do something about it. They can criticize and think that they will never fail themselves OR they can help bear that person's burden for the purpose of restoration. It's that simple!

The connection here is that when we hear of someone who has fallen, instead of running to their aid, we take the opportunity to talk bad about them and criticize them, because in our selfish mindset, we think that we are something, when really we are nothing, and we deceive (fool) ourselves! Our end will be much more painful and consequential than the brother or sister that just fell. May the Lord have mercy upon us all.

Neh'enah.

30

The Move of God! – Part 1

Moving by God's desires, promptings or wishes, is the key to a successful walk with God.

What I have discovered in my pursuit of God and in the endless task of discipling others to do the same, is that people are more interested in pursuing their own wishes, their own ambitions, and their own desires. Nothing to do with the will of the Father!

When following Christ, we are called to be quick to position ourselves so that we may hear Him and obey Him at all costs. This one thought is what divides the boys from the men and the girls from the women.

In my devotion today, I want to bring forth something that God has been revealing to me little by little. It's the way to attain success in the Lord and to move by God's divine order.

Now, when it comes to following the Lord, we are continually challenged to please the Lord with our decision-making. I do believe that there are different roads people take when pursuing the Lord's heart in obedience. Here are some:

The *Disciplined-Servant* Company: There are those that are very disciplined in their way of doing things; Everything they do is bathed with a disciplined mindset. This is a great thing to have in my opinion. These are usually the people that get the most done in any place and at any time. These servants of the Lord tend to be *very hard* on themselves and they leave no room for failure; they can't stand mediocrity either. Another added plus to these disciplined servants of God, is that they are self-starters. They take initiative in every area of their lives. When they read a command from the word of God, they don't ask, they just do it! Overall, being a disciplined individual is a big plus in any forum.

The *Waiting to be Told What to Do* Company: There is another group of individuals who are not self-starters, and nor are they quick to jump into anything. These are the servants of the Lord who are waiting around to be told what to do. Do you know some of these? They come *in bunches!* No exaggeration here. They will not obey anything on their own. As a matter of fact, you almost have to get upset at them for them to move. When it comes to obeying God's commands, they are not sure of themselves. Now, they love God, but not enough to jump in and sacrifice their own lives. They still love themselves too much to lay down anything costly for God!

Finally, we have the last group, **The *Prophetic Servant* Company.** This is the vessel of God who is waiting for the Holy Spirit's prompting, always looking at the weather patterns to change as a sign; there are even times when they will be gazing at the stars for a phenomenon to appear. These are God's prophetic people who are not afraid of men because they know how to stand before God. They will think prophetically, they will hear prophetically, they will speak prophetically, and they will move and act prophetically— these are the prophetic company of the Lord. Yes, they are ready to jump in at any given time and fulfill the wishes of the Father.

As I begin to unfold these truths on what a move of God entails, let me just say that every move of God begins with one man or one woman. The move of God is never a company of people, but rather an individual who is hungry to please God. It's always a prophetic man or woman who sees the glory of God and is convinced that they are called to manifest it into the world they live in!

Neh'enah.

31

The Move of God! – Part 2

In studying the moves of God throughout the Bible and throughout history, I have come to note the fact that God uses humanity to get His wishes done. He will always raise up a man or a woman to do His bidding. He always moves in the hearts of His people to align society or establish a testimony of His awesomeness in culture.

Though sometimes it may seem like God is far away from the wicked culture we live in, I have to say that the opposite is actually also true. The Lord is in the middle of the prayers of His people who are called by His name. He has not departed anywhere yet, as a matter of fact, God is right in the middle of what we call *a mess*. Yes, He is waiting and looking for a servant who will stand up for His name's sake!

I do believe that God is never taken by surprise by anything that might go wrong in this drunken world. He is always ready to move and change the conditions that surround us and bring us to a place of stability.

Let me take you to a few places in Scripture and show you what happens when a man is *tapped* by God to do a task for Him:

First of all, let's look at the man of God in 1 Kings 13.

The Man of God...

"And behold, a man of God went from Judah to Bethel by the word of the Lord, and Jeroboam stood by the altar to burn incense. Then he cried out against the altar by the word of the Lord, and said, 'O altar, altar! Thus says the Lord: Behold, a child, Josiah by name, shall be born to the house of David; and on you he shall sacrifice the priests of the high places who burn incense on you, and men's bones shall be burned on you.'

And he gave a sign the same day, saying, 'This *is* the sign which the Lord has spoken: Surely the altar shall split apart, and the ashes on it shall be poured out.'" (1 Kings 13:1-3)

Before us now, we have the story of a man of God with whom the Lord used to communicate to the wicked king Jeroboam (the king of Israel) a prophetic word.

When I think of God moving on the earth, I think of what He desires to do among society, with people, governments, and culture. God moves the heart of His servants with the intention of getting something done that affects our destiny. That is what I believe a move of God is — it is God's agenda being brought down to man with the intent to align them with His will.

The first thing we must realize here, is that the man of God came from Judah and visited Bethel, not through his own choice, but by the *word* of the Lord. Did he know that King Jeroboam was there getting ready to burn incense at the altar? I don't believe he knew but God certainly did!

As the king was getting ready to burn incense, the man of God broke through with a word from heaven, **"Then he cried out against the altar by the word of the Lord, and said, 'O altar, altar! Thus says the Lord:'Behold, a child, Josiah by name, shall be born to the house of David; and on you he shall sacrifice the priests of the high places who burn incense on you, and men's bones shall be burned on you.'"**

If you keep reading the story, the man of God was reprimanded by the king for speaking out against the altar at Bethel and truly against King Jeroboam and his dishonor towards Jehovah God. The good thing is that the man of God had the Lord on his side and was able to move in power against him.

When God speaks or commands one of His servants to take a message to someone — all that servant can do is either obey or disobey. We must know that the move of God is contingent upon our obedience!

When God speaks, we must be quick to move with God's heart. This is how a move of God is birthed in the earth.

Neh'enah.

32

The Move of God – Part 3

Here's a strange event sponsored by the Lord along with the intent to make His presence known to the whole world.

"Then the Lord saw that the wickedness of man *was* great in the earth, and *that* every intent of the thoughts of his heart *was* only evil continually. And the Lord was sorry that He had made man on the earth, and He was grieved in His heart. So the Lord said, 'I will destroy man whom I have created from the face of the earth, both man and beast, creeping thing and birds of the air, for I am sorry that I have made them.'

But Noah found grace in the eyes of the Lord." (Genesis 6:5-9)

I do believe that every move of God is initiated by some type of disorder in the world we live in. I don't believe the Lord is *out there* looking for something to do with His mighty power just for the sake of it.

As a matter of fact, as the Lord's eyes move to and fro upon the earth, He sees the sinful disorder and the chaos that rebellion against Him has caused, and He begins to plan how He will change the situation or situations.

Sometimes, God looks and sees the wickedness, other times, God will allow humanity to see the duress sin has brought and then positions Himself to be the answer. They will then cry out to God in desperation with unceasing incessant prayers and plead with God to move by His mighty power and change things!

To all this I say that God will not allow things to get so bent out of shape before He moves and makes or brings significant changes. This seemed to be the case in this one move of God.

The Scripture says something very interesting in verse 9. It says, **"But Noah found grace in the eyes of the Lord."**

God saw all humanity and saw that it had corrupted itself. Yes, it was time for God to move, but through whom? God decided to move through a man who God acknowledged as being graceful, and highly favored— his name was Noah.

There were others (other people) God could have used, yet none were as qualified and as regarded as graceful as Noah. When one seeks the favor of God, God will favor them and call them when He needs something done! God chose Noah because God favored him, nothing else!

Noah's Response to the Move of God!

Volume 6

In Genesis 6, we read about Noah's *external* conversation with God and how it all was laid out for Noah to follow…

"And God said to Noah, 'The end of all flesh has come before Me, for the earth is filled with violence through them; and behold, I will destroy them with the earth. Make yourself an ark of gopherwood; make rooms in the ark, and cover it inside and outside with pitch. And this is how you shall make it: The length of the ark *shall* be three hundred cubits, its width fifty cubits, and its height thirty cubits. You shall make a window for the ark, and you shall finish it to a cubit from above; and set the door of the ark in its side. You shall make it *with* lower, second, and third *decks*. And behold, I Myself am bringing floodwaters on the earth, to destroy from under heaven all flesh in which is the breath of life; everything that *is* on the earth shall die. But I will establish My covenant with you; and you shall go into the ark—you, your sons, your wife, and your sons' wives with you. And of every living thing of all flesh you shall bring two of every sort into the ark, to keep *them* alive with you; they shall be male and female. Of the birds after their kind, of animals after their kind, and of every creeping thing of the earth after its kind, two of every *kind* will come to you to keep *them* alive. And you shall take for yourself of all food that is eaten, and you shall gather it to yourself; and it shall be food for you and for them.'

Thus Noah did; according to all that God commanded

him, so he did." (Genesis 6:13-22)

As we read God's plan laid out for Noah, it all seems like it was no big deal. From the text, we only read, **"Thus Noah did; according to all that God commanded him, so he did."**

But was it really that easy? I mean, was there any emotion? Was there any doubt? Was there any fear? What really happened? Let's look deeper...

Moved with Godly Fear!

In Hebrews 11:7, the writer allows us to see behind the veil and into the spirit of the matter. **"By faith Noah, being divinely warned of things not yet seen, moved with godly fear, prepared an ark for the saving of his household..."**

Hebrews tells us a little of what Noah actually felt *internally* as he not only heard what God told him, but also how he reacted after hearing God's plan, **"he moved with godly fear."**

What does this mean? It means that when Noah heard God speak, he was deeply shaken to the core that it produced action in him.

This man would no longer rest in his comfortable bed as if nothing was wrong. He would no longer sleep peacefully like he used to. He would no longer use his time unproductively. No sir, this man would now never have just an ordinary life! Noah was to be burdened by the coming fury of God; he needed to move with *reverence,* knowing that God was about to change the known world through a flood of water like the world had never seen!

A move of God will always affect the man who God calls first. God will first reveal His heart and mind to the vessel, and then He will release or send that vessel into *the work*. To move with God's vision means that the vessel of God has caught a glimpse of what God is about to do and positions himself to be of any help to God.

Will you be the *move of God* on the earth to your generation?

Neh'enah.

33

The Move of God! – Part 4

Anytime that Jesus appears to us— by way of appearing in the Word of God as we meditate, through a preacher at our local church, or via a prophet with the gift to do personal prophecy, a personal change is ultimately inevitable.

Either we will receive God's word in our hearts and grow, or we will reject the opportunity to know God in deeper ways.

The Rich Young Ruler

Regarding the subject of the move of God, this is exactly what took place in this next passage: God moved towards an individual with His agenda, and the rich young man had to ponder a lot of things, before deciding to follow Christ. Read on…

"Now as He was going out on the road, one came running, knelt before Him, and asked Him, 'Good Teacher, what shall I do that I may inherit eternal life?' So Jesus said to him, 'Why do you call Me good? No one is good but One, *that is*, God. You know the commandments: *Do not commit adultery, Do not murder, Do not steal, Do not bear false witness, Do not defraud, Honor your father and*

your mother.'
And he answered and said to Him, 'Teacher, all these things I have kept from my youth.'
Then Jesus, looking at him, loved him, and said to him, 'One thing you lack: Go your way, sell whatever you have and give to the poor, and you will have treasure in heaven; and come, take up the cross, and follow Me.'
But he was sad at this word, and went away sorrowful, for he had great possessions."

The Scripture says that this one man came to Christ and knelt before Him, longing to know the answer to the million-dollar question, *what shall I do that I may inherit eternal life?*

The Move of God Begins Within Us First!

You see, the move of God first begins deep inside our hearts. Something deep inside this young ruler made him come to Christ. The prompting that this man felt was really God moving Him towards Christ. I do believe that every move of God starts with God!

After this man found Christ, the Lord then moved on Him. It was Christ who answered this young man's question by saying, **"You know the commandments: *Do not...*"**

As the Lord begins to move in our hearts with fresh revelation, we will be held accountable for what He is saying.

This is how the moves of God are birthed.

In the case of this young man who desired God's best, nothing was accomplished in the end. He didn't allow Christ to move in Him and thus the move of God ceased. Don't let this be you!

Peter Walks on Water!

"Immediately Jesus made His disciples get into the boat and go before Him to the other side, while He sent the multitudes away. And when He had sent the multitudes away, He went up on the mountain by Himself to pray. Now when evening came, He was alone there. But the boat was now in the middle of the sea, tossed by the waves, for the wind was contrary. Now in the fourth watch of the night Jesus went to them, walking on the sea. And when the disciples saw Him walking on the sea, they were troubled, saying, 'It is a ghost!'
And they cried out for fear. But immediately Jesus spoke to them, saying, 'Be of good cheer! It is I; do not be afraid.'
And Peter answered Him and said, 'Lord, if it is You, command me to come to You on the water.'
So He said, 'Come.'
And when Peter had come down out of the boat, he walked on the water to go to Jesus." (Matthew 14:17-29)

In our verses here, Peter was challenged to move with

God.

It was Christ who was walking on the water, but Peter didn't recognize Him at first. It was out of this opportunity that God decided to manifest Himself to Peter.

We again see that the move of God is not only progressive, but also that action is needed if you are going to manifest Christ to the world.

The move of God will always take us to the place where God needs us to be. Whether we are qualified to be in that place or not, God will make sure we are equipped as we go to that special place of obedience.

Once we move with God, we will become the expression God is looking for. To sum up: the move of God begins with us first, and then others will join in! Get ready to bring the move of God into your life first, then your family, then into your workplace, your school, and your ministry.

Neh'enah.

34

The Spirit of Corruption!

"Flesh gives birth to flesh, but the Spirit gives birth to spirit." (John 3:6)

"Whoever sows to please their flesh, from the flesh will reap destruction; whoever sows to please the Spirit, from the Spirit will reap eternal life." (Galatians 6:8)

In my pursuit to understand this topic in a deeper way, I want to share with you my own heart experience…

Born in the Flesh!

As we come into this world, the obvious thing to say is that we are born in sin and every act from that point on will be tainted by our sinful nature, *our flesh*. When I am speaking of the flesh, I am speaking about our carnal nature. I am speaking of that horrible thing that you and I are bound to from birth.

Now, most civilized people tend to behave normally, provided there is nothing provoking that ugly beast that lives with us. Yes, that latent beast that has the potential to come forth and cause havoc at any given time or place.

Many years ago, I met this pastor who told me about a specific woman in his congregation. He mentioned her because of some good deeds she had done, and I was praising her for her willingness to serve and be a tool in God's hand. Immediately this pastor told me, *The only thing about this woman, is that if you press the wrong button with her, she will give you a piece of her mind.* I laughed, but he didn't. Apparently, this individual had been in some scuffles with other members of her church, and she was known as a troublemaker! Do you know people like this?

When she was in a good mood, she was a saint, and when she was not having a great day, she would become an unpleasant person, and yes, I am putting it mildly.

It would be good to note here that we must make every effort to live above reproach so that people don't brand us as two-faced hypocrites. We who walk in the Spirit of the Lord are held to a higher order.

Maintained by the Flesh

People who tend to walk in the flesh must continue feeding this lifestyle. They will feed their fleshly thoughts and emotions, and do things that make themselves feel good, appreciated, and aggrandized.

Is it any wonder that personal prayer is the last of spiritual exercises sought after in the local church? In the church world, people get excited about their worship teams, their outreaches, their service to the community, – but I have yet to hear someone say, *Our prayer meeting has been amazing. Our night watches have truly challenged us as God has been revealing His heart to us!*

The flesh will always look for comfort. It will hide behind good deeds, so long as it is being praised by people. The flesh will run away from anything that sounds like discipline, death, or giving of itself in exchange for God's will.

I always marvel when Christians say, *We are going to this Christian concert, so and so is going to be there! It's only $20.00 to get in.*

If I question the motive of why they are going or what they are really looking for, they will always answer in a very spiritual tone and say, *More of Jesus brother! Just want more of Him.*

Doesn't this sound noble and spiritual? Well of course it does! So, my reply is always the same: *If you want more of Jesus, come and join me at the prayer meeting at 5am. Come and meet Christ the Lord in person. Oh and by the way, it is free of charge!*

Ask me if they come....I think you know the answer to that. Their flesh will not allow them to come and die to their flesh at the feet of Jesus! Are you kidding me?

The Embarrassing Results of the Flesh!

"Whoever sows to please their flesh, from the flesh will reap destruction; whoever sows to please the Spirit, from the Spirit will reap eternal life." (Galatians 6:8)

If we continue pleasing or appeasing the flesh, the Scripture says that the results will be embarrassing. The flesh has an alluring effect, and it will suck people into its grasp! It will use and abuse the person who is led by it.

After the flesh does its perfect work, it will leave you and I full of shame and embarrassed in the sight of those who could see it but never dared to say anything about it.

In this one verse in Galatians 6:8, Paul says that whoever sows to please their flesh, from the flesh they will reap corruption. The end of it all will be catastrophic. I speak as a fool and one with experience of this truth.

The fact here is that God will *not* allow you or me to get away with anything! You might try to be very suave, sharp, or think that you are smarter than the *next person*, but let me tell you….the flesh is no respecter of persons — it is a ravaging fire, and it will consume you and anyone who is led by it!

In closing, the Apostle Paul, gives us the solution to overcoming this horrible power of the flesh. This is what Paul says, **"I say then: Walk in the Spirit, and you shall not fulfill the lust of the flesh."** (Galatians 5:16)

In prayer every morning, spend time with God. Get in the Spirit of the Lord. Allow the Spirit of God to fill your life thoroughly. Invite Him to flood your soul with His presence daily. Don't leave home without it!

Neh'enah.

35

How Spiritual Am I?

"Who *is* this coming up from the wilderness, Leaning upon her beloved?" (Song of Solomon 8:5)

Have you ever found yourself being tested beyond your own capacity and completely unable to deal with the trial at hand? There are tests for the believer that come in an array of ways, but there are also those tests that have been given or should I say, *reserved*, for those God has appointed for something more specific.

Obviously, when one is being tested, it is hard to see the hand of God introducing anything *that* painful in our lives. Well, to your surprise and mine, God does release tempest and storms into our lives for the purpose of producing spiritual ascendency (authority, dominion) in us!

There is no way you can talk about leaning upon your Beloved, if you have never had to *lean* on Him in a practical way! There is no way for you to know what it means for God to put His hand under your head and embrace you, (read Songs of Solomon 8:3) if you have never been to this place in God!

It's Time to Face Your Storm!

"Those who go down to the sea in ships,
Who do business on great waters,
They see the works of the Lord,
And His wonders in the deep.
For He commands and raises the stormy wind,
Which lifts up the waves of the sea.
They mount up to the heavens,
They go down again to the depths;
Their soul melts because of trouble.
They reel to and fro, and stagger like a drunken man,
And are at their wits' end.
Then they cry out to the Lord in their trouble,
And He brings them out of their distresses.
He calms the storm,
So that its waves are still.
Then they are glad because they are quiet;
So He guides them to their desired haven." (Psalm 107-23-30)

Unlike other teachings and doctrines that I have heard, I believe that all storms come from the Lord and for the Lord's purposes. There is nothing that happens to us, His children that God has not ordained!

In the midst of your own tempest, yes, the kind where you don't know if you are coming or going, the ones that seem to be like night that never ends or a frigid cold winter with no one to provide any warmth for you— the *spiritual* tsunami that comes to you is unexpected and leaves you alone to pick up the pieces after it passes. Yes, these storms all come from the Lord!

It's all About Your Spiritual Posture!

I don't claim to have all the answers to life's storms, but one thing I have learned in God is that once the storm passes, once the wintertime passes, in some strange way, it all becomes beautiful in His time.

Now, in my experience of going through some storms in my own walk, I must ask myself, **What was my posture spiritually, emotionally, or mentally, after the storm passed? Where will I be once the storm is passed? Will I be standing? Will I be begging? Will I be injured? Will I be bitter? Will I be better? Will I be found away from the Lord, or will I be found leaning upon my Beloved?**

I do believe that God wants to bring us into storms for multiple purposes:

Spiritual Ascendency: The Lord wants to take us through some storms to develop spiritual authority in our lives. You can't give what you don't have….so the Lord invites us to have so we can give.

Patience and Perseverance: I believe God uses tests and trials to teach us patience and perseverance. These two things are qualities that we must apprehend in our own walk of faith. Can you believe God until…until He brings the breakthrough?

Spiritual Posture: Where will the storm leave you? Running away from God, complaining to God, whining to God, or leaning upon Him?

May the Spirit of the Lord continue to guide us in our journey, and may we prove ourselves faithful during the fiercest storm. Remember, it is the Lord who holds the cup of testing *[Read John 18:11 for clarity, if needed.]*

Neh'enah.

36

Beware of Christianity-Lite! - Part 1

**"Woe to the rebellious children, says the Lord,
Who take counsel, but not of Me,
And who devise plans, but not of My Spirit,
That they may add sin to sin;
Who walk to go down to Egypt,
And have not asked My advice,
To strengthen themselves in the strength of Pharaoh,
And to trust in the shadow of Egypt!
Therefore the strength of Pharaoh
Shall be your shame,
And trust in the shadow of Egypt
Shall be *your* humiliation."** (Isaiah 30:1-3)

In my prayer time this week, I came across these passages of scripture from the Book of Isaiah, and let me tell you, I felt the Spirit of the Lord speaking loud and clear yet one more time!

I want to share some of my findings about how the Lord longs for us to become aligned with His heart. People still think that going to church is all that they need to do, but let me tell you, going to church without God's presence in your life, will only make you religious. You are no better than the drunk that lives down the street.

Why the Title?

Let me start by saying that the main reason I gave these next few meditations the title *Beware of Christianity-Lite*, is for the simple reason that too many believers today are flocking to churches for nothing more than just a good *spiritual ear-tickling* that has nothing to do with the holiness of God and what living for Jesus is all about.

Rebellious Children!

In the Book of Isaiah, we find God's heart one more time *broken* over the rebellious children of Israel.

**"Woe to the rebellious children, says the Lord,
Who take counsel, but not of Me,
And who devise plans, but not of My Spirit,
That they may add sin to sin…"**

There is a group of so-called Christian followers who are not in tune with God but with self! Their motive is not about pleasing Christ, but rather themselves! I have met too many of these servants. Yes, they appear humble, noble, and spiritual, yet they don't know Christ in the way He longs for them to know Him!

They always want to do good, but they don't seek counsel from the Lord. No sir, they seek counsel from people who are just like them. They have the same spirit that their drinking buddies have— they are as fleshly as the rebellious person next to them.

I think it's very interesting that in the Book of Isaiah, it says that these rebellious children keep devising plans, but nothing to do with the Spirit of God. In other words, they are led by a spirit, but it is not the Holy Spirit! It's a fleshly spirit that only leads them to commit sin after sin.

Enslaved by Another System!

**"Who walk to go down to Egypt,
And have not asked My advice,
To strengthen themselves in the strength of Pharaoh,
And to trust in the shadow of Egypt!"**

These so-called believers all do the same stuff and practice the same methods as worldly people do. The Scripture adds that these rebellious children tend to go down to Egypt and find strength in *Pharoah's world*.

Egypt represents *the world*, and Pharaoh is the head of this world. In short, it's the believer finding refuge in the flesh, the devil, or the world, if you will. There is no confusing the message here: Carnal or fleshly so-called believers are enamored with this world system! They say no, but their lifestyle says otherwise.

To close this first part, let us see the consequence of those who follow Pharaoh's world:

**"Therefore the strength of Pharaoh
Shall be your shame,
And trust in the shadow of Egypt
Shall be *your* humiliation."**

As you can see, this whole way of living and compromising our walk with Christ will end up in shame and humiliation. It may take a while before we are put to shame due to our rebellion, but it will nevertheless come in due season.

Just because we don't see divine retribution now, doesn't mean that it is not on its way! If we reap into the flesh (without fail) we will reap corruption! Let us lay it down: either this principle is true, or God is a liar! I doubt that God is lying!

Neh'enah.

37

Beware of Christianity-Lite! - Part 2

"That this *is* a rebellious people,
Lying children,
Children *who* will not hear the law of the Lord;
Who say to the seers, 'Do not see,'

And to the prophets, 'Do not prophesy to us right things;
Speak to us smooth things, prophesy deceits.
Get out of the way,
Turn aside from the path,
Cause the Holy One of Israel
To cease from before us.'" (Isaiah 30:8-11)

I heard a Christian brother one time say that God doesn't look outward but rather, He sees us internally. There is really no point of argument for this, and no one should argue this point. The only problem with this is that our lives are surrounded by people! It is other people who see us. It is others who see our expressions, albeit good or bad. Do you get me?

The testimony of individuals will always be under a microscope by those who surround them. It will be the people who surround us who will be the judges of our actions, not God. As far as our hearts being pure before God, there may be no question about that. As far as our actions before others — this is where the real question lies.

The Fine Line

When walking with the Lord, there are many *fine lines* that people tend to border on. Some cross them daily, some still hold back, nevertheless, many believers like to live on the fence. Not fully in with God, but not fully out of alignment with God.

When life brings about difficulty, some believers run towards God. When things are going well, they tend to slack off and lend themselves to the world and its pleasures. Mind you, it is not a lot that they allow themselves to indulge in worldly pleasure— it's only a little bit! Yet, this little bit is what has brought much of the disgrace in God's people.

Let me reiterate a portion of the Scriptures that I used as a text for this devotion. Here's a part of it:

"That this *is* a rebellious people,
Lying children,
Children *who* will not hear the law of the Lord."

The Lord concludes one matter: His people are rebellious and liars. If this wasn't enough, the Lord continues to say that they just won't hear the law of the Lord.

Please note: God's children kept a form of religion. Yes, they still attended the ceremonies, kept the feasts, dressed the part, and to some degree reviewed God's words. All this to no avail. Their heart was not in it! They couldn't wait to get out of the synagogue to go and do their own thing! Maybe some people didn't know it, or they couldn't tell that they were being rebellious and selfish — yet God could tell!

Pillow Prophets!

Another interesting point I would like to address in my devotion is that God's people really didn't want to be corrected. Remember, God used His holy prophets to bring in a word of correction to God's people as needed. Listen to this:

"And to the prophets, 'Do not prophesy to us right things; Speak to us smooth things, prophesy deceits.'"

These rebellious "church people" simply wanted someone to tickle their ears and make them happy. They didn't want God's holy words! They wanted pillow prophets to give them something soft and fleshly.

They would make their requests known by telling the prophets, **"Do not prophesy to us right things; speak to us smooth things, prophesy deceits."**

I believe that today's believers have great tendencies to be led by their flesh more than ever before in the history of the church. They want to be spoken to with smooth things. They don't want to be challenged to follow Jesus all the way!

It is my humble opinion that today's church has made it so accommodating for the fleshly people to come and be part of "God's group" without repentance and a pursuit for holiness. What a mockery to the cross of Christ!

As I close this section of Christianity-*lite*, let me just say to you, His follower: Don't ever look for the easy road to following Jesus! This method of following Christ is not of the Lord and of His Spirit. It is pure flesh and self-aggrandizing.

Neh'enah.

38

Beware of Christianity-Lite! - Part 3

"In returning and rest you shall be saved;
In quietness and confidence shall be your strength.

But you would not,
And you said, 'No, for we will flee on horses'"—

Therefore you shall flee!
And, 'We will ride on swift *horses*'—
Therefore those who pursue you shall be swift!" (Isaiah 30:15, 16)

As I come to the third part of my devotion, *Beware of Christianity-Lite!* — I have to say that God knew that His people would always waver between two opinions. God knew that His people were only as loyal as they made claims to be — He knew that they would eventually falter.

In knowing this, God always made provision for His people to return to Him. He always gave second chances and sometimes even more than that.

In studying these few Scriptures, I discovered that God's people were very rebellious in their hearts against the Lord. Due to their degree of selfishness (which propelled them over the edge) they would do things without keeping in mind the standards of the Lord. The ancient landmarks of moral living were nonexistent! Way too often, the people of God tempted the Lord's goodness and mercy, until the Lord released His judgment upon them.

The Return

It was through the Prophet Isaiah that the Lord said to His people:
"In returning and rest you shall be saved;
In quietness and confidence shall be your strength."

There is an interesting thing here that I want you to observe. I want you to see how God promised His people if they returned and found rest in Him, they would be saved. He would provide a refuge for them!

Once we find rest in Him, we will enter a quietness in our spirit and a confidence that will be supernatural. It is these elements that will give us strength to overcome anything.

But You Would Not!

"But you would not,
And you said, 'No, for we will flee on horses'—

Therefore you shall flee!
And, 'We will ride on swift *horses*'—

Therefore those who pursue you shall be swift!"

You know that the level of rebellion among God's people was very high. They didn't want anything to do with God! When God made provision for them, they simply said, **"No, for we will flee on horses — we will ride on swift horses."**

To this the Lord replied two things:

First: Yes, they would be fleeing from the enemy, and secondly, those pursuing them would also be swift. Do you see this? To the degree that we are rebellious is to the degree that the enemy will be with us. If we are swift to disobey, the enemy will be swift to do their work on us. To the degree we run away, is to the degree we will be captured!

Let me close this devotion by saying that unless there is a repentant heart in us, we won't find our way back to God. We will always be fleeing but never getting away from no one!

If we repent, then God will even make our enemies be at peace with us!

"When a man's ways please the LORD, He makes even his enemies to be at peace with him." (Proverbs 16:7)

Neh'enah.

39

Glorifying the Father!

"By this My Father is glorified, that you bear much fruit; so you will be My disciples." (John 15:8)

"Then one of them, a lawyer, asked *Him* a question, testing Him, and saying, 'Teacher, which is the great commandment in the law?'

Jesus said to him, 'You shall love the Lord your God with all your heart, with all your soul, and with all your mind. This is the first and great commandment. And the second is like it: You shall love your neighbor as yourself.'

On these two commandments hang all the Law and the Prophets." (Matthew 22:35-40)

When we make any reference to what it means *to bear fruit* in the kingdom of God, what exactly are we referring to? Apparently, those who have been following Christ have been likened to trees planted near rivers of water, and due to their location they will bear fruit in its season.

It would be safe to say that once anyone has been planted, they will eventually produce fruit in due season. The fruit will come forth providing that the tree is free from bugs, insects, or an infestation eating away at its new shoots.

Let me also add that a healthy tree will for the most part be productive and produce good fruit.

What About Us?

As believers and followers of Christ, we also are called to bear fruit. The fruit that comes forth from us will speak loud and clear— those around us will give testimony of praise. It is at this point that the heavenly Father is glorified!

Now, how do we become healthy *spiritual* trees? How does our life bring glory to our heavenly Father daily? What things must be done to cultivate our lives and make sure that we are healthy trees producing God-honoring and God-glorifying fruit?

It's All in the Cultivation!

In the Scripture that I used above regarding the two greatest commandments; we will find the secret of becoming a good healthy spiritual tree.

If we are to become healthy spiritual trees, we must first understand the way God produces fruit in us. Remember, all trees start with a seed. If there is no seed, there will be no tree. Christ in us is the seed.

We must cultivate this seed that is deep within us. Remember, this seed is in our hearts and it can only be attended to by an intimate relationship with God. Here's what Jesus said, **"You shall love the Lord your God with all your heart, with all your soul, and with all your mind. This is the first and great commandment."**

If this part of our cultivation doesn't exist, or doesn't take place, we might as well forget about this tree growing and much less produce any fruit! An intimate life with God is a huge prerequisite if our tree is ever to grow. Taking time to meet God in prayer and allowing ourselves to fall in love with Him daily will always be the key that makes the spiritual tree grow.

The Fruit Will Always Be Contingent Upon the Health of the Tree!

As we spend time with God and allow Him to take over our lives, His Spirit will take us to places we have never known; He will carry us into opportunities that we could only have dreamed of.

Jesus said, **"You shall love your neighbor as yourself."**

It is interesting to notice that Christ first spoke of the first commandment as us loving Him with all we have. This was the first commandment. It is obvious to me that without a tree, there cannot be any fruit.

We must first focus on the tree and its health. Secondly, we must turn our attention to the fruit that it will produce and all its possibilities. When the right time for that tree to produce fruit comes, it will be ready to make its impact!

The experience with God must first be internal. Cultivating a personal relationship with God is a sure guarantee of good fruit soon. If the process takes place, it will work its magic and give us what we desire.

Remember: Sweet fruit will always leave an exceptional and lasting expression. It is this what glorifies the Father!

Neh'enah.

40

God's Atomic Power! - Part 1

"For this purpose, the Son of God was manifested, that He might destroy the works of the devil." (1 John 3:8b)

As of late, I have been meditating on the benefits that Christians have received by virtue of receiving Christ into their hearts.

The blessing of knowing God has so much to it, that too many believers have become content with the little that they have received. God has promised to give His people all that they need to overcome. He has provided authority over all the works of the devil.

The only problem I see here is that too many believers don't know all that they have within themselves to carry out God's wishes!

God's Original Plan

God had an original plan, an original intent, if you will. His desire was to fill man with His glory and have him demonstrate it to the universe. The plan was to be carried out by His first created beings — Adam and Eve.

The plan was set into motion when the Lord created the Garden of Eden and placed man in it. He placed Adam and Eve and told them to take care and cultivate the garden. Along with this task given to them, He also gave them instructions of what not to do.

It was here where their devotion was tested. The serpent (the devil) appeared in this garden of Eden, and challenged God's servants to take and eat of this *forbidden* fruit. After giving it some thought, Eve took and ate some of the fruit and gave some to Adam. It was here, where sin came into the world and the benefits of a great life were taken away by the usurper, Satan. Man was tested and failed!

From this point forward, humanity was undone. They carried with them the guilt and shame brought on by their failure. Day in and day out, this burden was heavy upon them. God's justice had to take effect and was put into play when both of them were taken out of the garden of Eden.

This was God's way of saying to man, *You can't have it both ways! You can't have life and death at the same time!* The Lord acted by taking man out of the garden and allowing them to figure life out on their own without the guidance of the Holy Spirit.

God's Love in Motion!

Due to the failure of humanity, one would think that God had given up on His creation, but nothing could be further from the truth!

In Genesis 3:15, the Lord prophesied of a coming day when the serpent's head would be crushed by the heel of God!

"And I will put enmity
Between you and the woman,
And between your seed and her Seed;
He shall bruise your head,
And you shall bruise His heel." (Genesis 3:15)

The Lord began a move that would change the whole spiritual landscape of humanity by setting in motion a redemption plan that He designed before the foundations of the world were created.

It was to be a move that would make every demon in hell tremble and run for their lives!

The Devil Waits and Wonders!

From the day that God prophesied in Genesis 3:15, the devil has been waiting and wondering when this *crushing* will come to pass. I am sure he is trying to figure it all out by hearing the prophets speak, by watching the stars, by hearing the rabbis at the local synagogue, etc.

To close this first part of my devotion, I would like for you to keep in mind that no one knows the mind of God except the Spirit of God. If the Lord has spoken to you, consider yourself special. It is this seed that you have inside that the devil wants to abort. Once He knows that there is an intent, He will attack! All to stop the *crushing of his head*!

Neh'enah.

41

God's Atomic Power - Part 2

"Now after Jesus was born in Bethlehem of Judea in the days of Herod the king, behold, wise men from the East came to Jerusalem, saying, 'Where is He who has been born King of the Jews? For we have seen His star in the East and have come to worship Him.'
When Herod the king heard *this*, he was troubled, and all Jerusalem with him. And when he had gathered all the chief priests and scribes of the people together, he inquired of them where the Christ was to be born.

So, they said to him, 'In Bethlehem of Judea, for thus it is written by the prophet:

But you, Bethlehem, in the land of Judah,
Are not the least among the rulers of Judah;
For out of you shall come a Ruler
Who will shepherd My people Israel.'" (Matthew 2:1-6)

The Deposit!

Once the devil knows that you are carrying God within you, the devil himself will make sure to silence and kill this passion.

Don't be fooled by putting your trust in your emotions; the devil means business and he is not playing games with you.

Don't allow pride and arrogance to set you up for failure!

It is vital for the servant of God to understand the value of what God has deposited within.

Changed by Responsibility!

I noticed how people behave when they don't have any responsibility in their lives. They live loosely, carelessly, and don't feel accountable to anyone.

Once an individual takes on responsibility, you will see that person transform before your very eyes. They will become more disciplined, more sensitive, more aware of their surroundings, more attentive to situations, and more responsible with the things that affect them personally.

When a woman becomes pregnant, she changes her pace in life. She becomes more aware of her health and well-being in general. When the seed comes, expansion in the mindset should accompany it.

When the devil found out that Mary, who was to be married to Joseph, was pregnant with a child, he wondered why this baby was so important.

Before John the Baptist announced and pointed out the Lamb of God who would take away the sins of the world — the wise men from the East were already on their way to affirm the new-born king at Bethlehem.

In God's Timing!

In the Spirit of the Lord, not even the devil knows where God is going with His awesome plan. He can only wonder but has no clue of anything God has in store!

When God is ready to move, there is no power in hell to stop Him.

The devil couldn't stop this baby from being born, though he tried. He couldn't convince Mary (the virgin) to say, *No, I don't want God to use my womb.* The Devil couldn't stop the angel from prophesying to Mary, and much less stop the spirit from overshadowing her and impregnating her.

Once the Lord decides to move, there is no stopping Him! Amen.

Neh'enah.

42

God's Atomic Power - Part 3

"When they had twisted a crown of thorns, they put *it* on His head, and a reed in His right hand. And they bowed the knee before Him and mocked Him, saying, 'Hail, King of the Jews!'

Then they spat on Him and took the reed and struck Him on the head. And when they had mocked Him, they took the robe off Him, put His *own* clothes on Him, and led Him away to be crucified." (Matthew 27:29-31)

It is interesting to notice how the devil truly feels about God, His plans, and His vessels. Make no mistake about this: the devil hates God and all that God has planned to do on behalf of His creation.

There is no wonder why the devil makes every effort to stop those whom God has called an anointed to do His bidding. He doesn't want the kingdom of God to advance or to make any type of impact upon the earth.

Satan is forever demeaning, discrediting, and discouraging the move of God upon the earth.

The Devil's Method

The believer – God's chosen vessel. The Devil will move in on the vessel first. Though the call of God is powerful and sure, and though the anointing of the Holy Spirit is real and vibrant on the vessel's life, the vessel of God still has a great responsibility to walk in God's ways!

Making the right choices, the godly choices, is the real secret to this victorious life in God.

If the believer is focused on Christ, if His heart is pursuing the Lord's desires, the enemy doesn't stand a chance against God.

It is amazing that God has placed the responsibility upon the believers and not on Himself. Yes, it is up to the vessel of God to respond correctly against the wiles of the enemy.

The second way the devil makes an attempt to stop the believer of Christ is through external means. The devil can't touch the man of God, but he can try to scare him with external forces. Often the enemy will raise up people against God's servants, this is done to hinder or stop the believer from advancing.

Trust me, the enemy is very well informed of who you are. *The anointing you have within you has been announced to the whole earth* [Job 2:2, 3].

If God has touched you, the devil has your number [Acts 19:15]!

Often due to personal failure, the devil will bring discouragement to the vessel of God. He will bring guilt, shame, and feelings of unworthiness and inadequacies.

We, as vessels of God, must continue to rely upon our identity in Christ, and the prophetic call of God our lives. These are powerful weapons given to us by the Lord Himself— and yes, here's where the call that is upon our lives gets its atomic power— the power to sustain us and bring us out of any adversity and into His glory!

Neh'enah.

43

God's Atomic Power - Part 4

"But the angel answered and said to the women, 'Do not be afraid, for I know that you seek Jesus who was crucified. He is not here; for He is risen, as He said.'" (Matthew 27:5, 6)

Just when the enemy thought that He had defeated and done away with God's eternal plan, Christ, by the power of the Spirit, was raised from the dead!

Jesus was not to be denied His resurrection. The devil couldn't stop Him, the grave couldn't hold Him, the guards couldn't keep Him from coming out of the tomb, Hell had only one choice — give back the keys to its rightful Owner!

The victory that Christ gained at Calvary and the resurrection from death, will forever mark the foundation and base for our Christian faith. We will always have this event to look back to and cling to, as God's way of giving us the atomic power and authority over darkness — forever!

God's Pattern for the Believer

God gave us believers this authority over darkness; we

carry it within our hearts and minds. The Spirit of the Lord that dwells within us is more powerful than anything created; it is more powerful than any spiritual force arrayed against the believer.

To add to these facts: If any person in any place at any time calls upon the Lord Jesus for salvation, the Lord will hear Him and deliver Him from all spiritual forces of darkness and set Him free to worship Him.

The Resurrection Did Happen!

"Now if Christ is preached that He has been raised from the dead, how do some among you say that there is no resurrection of the dead? But if there is no resurrection of the dead, then Christ is not risen. And if Christ is not risen, then our preaching is empty, and your faith *is* also empty. Yes, and we are found false witnesses of God because we have testified of God that He raised up Christ, whom He did not raise up—if in fact the dead do not rise. For if *the* dead do not rise, then Christ is not risen. And if Christ is not risen, your faith *is* futile; you are still in your sins! Then also those who have fallen asleep in Christ have perished. If in this life only we have hope in Christ, we are of all men the most pitiable. But now Christ is risen from the dead, *and* has become the first fruits of those who have fallen asleep." (1 Corinthians 15:12-21)

For all who would doubt that Christ rose from the dead, I must say, there is really no hope for you if you do not believe in the resurrection.

Wouldn't the devil love to have us believe this? Of course. Let me close this devotion by saying that God's atomic power rests upon His resurrection. If Christ rose from the dead, then we too, have risen to walk in the same power! Don't let the devil tell you that Christ has not risen and that you are hopeless without any help. The devil is a liar and the father of lies.

"...as He said!"

"He is not here; for He is risen, as He said."

It is time to appropriate ourselves for this power. King Jesus is alive and well. He has risen just as He said. Jesus has paid the full price, and we stand in power because of His finished work!

Neh'enah.

Volume 6

44

God's Atomic Power - Part 5

"**But you are not in the flesh but in the Spirit, if indeed the Spirit of God dwells in you. Now if anyone does not have the Spirit of Christ, he is not His. And if Christ *is* in you, the body *is* dead because of sin, but the Spirit *is* life because of righteousness. But if the Spirit of Him who raised Jesus from the dead dwells in you, He who raised Christ from the dead will also give life to your mortal bodies through His Spirit who dwells in you.**" (Romans 8:9-11)

Potential Power!

How powerful is the new birth? How strong are those who have died to self and embraced the cross of Christ? Well, I really don't know the potential of that, but here is what I know: Those who have experienced Christ are only as strong as their faith (the faith of God) that can be downloaded from God's throne room upon their hearts!

This specific faith is contingent upon our belief that we can receive it, for God gives it without holding back to all who dare to believe God for the impossible!

God's Atomic Power Is . . .

Now, God's *atomic power* is the Spirit of God! Here's a wild thought: To think that the Creator of the universe has made us partakers of this power is an awesome thought, but even more *mind-blowing*, is the reality that this power is made resident in our very hearts!

When this power is flowing in us, it revitalizes our natural being, it vivifies our mortal body to align with God's heart and will. Yes, when the Spirit of the Lord comes upon us and makes its home in us, we will do supernatural stuff! Thank God for His gentle Spirit.

Now That He Dwells Within

Now that the Spirit of God dwells within, what can we expect from Him?

Let's just say, for starters, the very nature of Christ has taken root within us and will begin to manifest its sweet-smelling aroma of life everywhere it goes. Though His Spirit is within us, it will glow through our countenance; it can be seen for miles. Also, the Spirit of God working within us will be felt by those who surround us. When we speak or pray for someone, the Spirit of God will be released with intention to heal and glorify Christ.

The Testimony of Life

God's *atomic power* is embedded in the very essence of the

life of Christ, which dwells richly in us. Make no mistake about this. If you have been born-again of the Spirit of God, then you have tasted of God's goodness and of the power of the age that is to come!

The glory of God will be upon you and *hell* will tremble at the sight of you. Go forth in His Name and do signs and wonders. For the Lord Himself will be with you for He will be in you! Now, this is atomic power 101.

Neh'enah.

45

God's Atomic Power - Part 6

"**Jesus answered and said to him, 'If anyone loves Me, he will keep My word; and My Father will love him, and We will come to him and make Our home with him.'** (John 14:23)

When I think of the possibilities of this atomic power, I also think of the wonderful experience of Christ coming to reside in me and be in me till the end of the age! Wow.

Jesus said that if I allowed Him to dwell in me and keep His words, that He and the Father would come and make their home in me— do you understand the magnitude of this?

Do you understand all that this experience entails, and how it affects us personally? Let's look at it.

If Christ comes to live within, that means that all that He is, can *potentially* be carried out in us. All that Christ represented on the earth, we can also represent. The power that resided in Him in bodily form, *now* resides in us!

Atomic Power Is Ours!

As we come to Christ, He comes to live in us. This unlocks so many things that favor us.

Now for starters, God's atomic power includes two dimensions of His working in us: the fruit of the Spirit which works in our inward parts. Here's where our personal character is developed and refined. The gifts of the Spirit, which are God's gifts to the servant of Christ are designed to help us move in God's power (signs and wonders included) upon the earth.

Let's look at the fruit of the Spirit first...

Fruit of the Spirit

"But the fruit of the Spirit is love, joy, peace, longsuffering, kindness, goodness, faithfulness, gentleness, self-control. Against such there is no law." (Galatians 5:22, 23)

When the Spirit of the Lord comes to live within, the first thing the Spirit does in us is show us the character of Christ. It teaches us who Christ is. It not only educates us mentally, but travels to the very core of our inner being and educates us in a deep spiritual way.

The training is carried out by the things we suffer. Enemies of all sorts, adverse situations, personal struggles, and how we deal with fiery trials are all part of God's training program to develop the character of Christ in us.

When being tested by God, don't run, don't whine, and don't complain! Stay put and drink the cup of pain. It's God holding the cup! You must know that this is God's way of developing a deeper longing for Him; a method to transform the old you into the new you made in the likeness of Christ. Allow God to complete His work in you!

Also, you must know that the fruit of the Spirit is developed by testing — it is not like a gift of the Spirit, which God also gives. The fruit of God's Spirit is developed slowly but surely as we abide in Him and He in us.

"...love, joy, peace, longsuffering, kindness, goodness, faithfulness, gentleness, self-control" — all these wonderful characteristics of Christ will be formed in us as we allow Christ to work a deep work through the things we suffer.

Neh'enah.

46

God's Atomic Power – Part 7

"Now concerning spiritual *gifts*, brethren, I do not want you to be ignorant…" (I Corinthians 12:1)

Allow me to continue our devotion from the last chapter where I began to unveil the wonderful revelation of what it is to walk in God's atomic power and allow Him to make His home in us.

The promises that we have in Christ and in the Father are truly so powerful and out of this world.

In the last devotion, I spoke about the fruit of the Spirit and made an application to its development and how we can become more Christ-like by allowing Him to rule in us, even when we are being tested in a fiery furnace.

Let's look at the other dimension of God's power as we look into the Gifts of the Spirit…

Gifts of the Spirit

In 1 Corinthians 12:1, the Apostle Paul makes it a point to inform the believers of this awesome gifting that we find in the Spirit of God. Anyone who walks with God can avail themselves of these spiritual gifts by simply asking God for them. You don't have to be a super Christian per se to receive these wonderful tools for ministering to others.

When we speak of God's atomic power, we are including these wonderful gifts that God has prepared for anyone who desires them. It is by the manifestation of God's gifts in the lives of people, that His presence is made known.

Please know that *the world* is looking for this kind of power. Of course, people who are without Christ want to know about their own future and the future in general. Of course, the people without Christ want to know about the supernatural things that happen in this life! God has gifted His people to have a powerful testimony among *the lost*.

Here are the 9 gifts of the Spirit as outlined in 1 Corinthians 12:1-11:

The Word of Wisdom: A supernatural revelation or insight into the divine will and purpose, often given by the Spirit to solve perplexing problems and situations.

The Word of Knowledge: The Word of Knowledge is a supernatural revelation of Divine knowledge or insight in the Divine mind, will or plan, to know things that could not be known of oneself.

Discerning of Spirits: This is a supernatural revelation or insight into the realm of spirits to detect their presence and plans.

Prophecy: Prophecy is the supernatural utterance in the native tongue. It is a miracle of divine utterance, not conceived by human thought or reasoning. It includes speaking unto others: edification, exhortation, and comfort.

Divers Kinds of Tongues: The supernatural utterance in other languages that are not known to the speaker.

The Interpretation of Tongues: The supernatural ability to interpret in the native tongue what is uttered in other languages not known by the one who interprets by the Spirit.

Gift of Faith: This is a supernatural ability to believe God without human doubt, unbelief, or reasonings.

The Gift of Healing: The healing of all manner of sickness by supernatural power without human aid or medicine.

The Working of Miracles: Is supernatural power to intervene in the ordinary course of nature and to counteract natural laws if necessary.

As we walk in Christ's power, these gifts can potentially be manifested through those who believe — that would be us. Get ready to move in atomic power for His glory!

47

God's Atomic Power - Part 8

"But you shall receive power when the Holy Spirit has come upon you; and you shall be witnesses to Me in Jerusalem, and in all Judea and Samaria, and to the end of the earth." (Acts 1:8)

Why is it that our natural tendency is to be content with *so little* of the Lord and not pursue all that He has for us? We become easily satisfied with meeting once a week at church and we don't spend time at God's altar like we know we should.

Our personal prayer life is non-existent or spiritually dry at best. Our spiritual appetite is only provoked by an atmosphere of worship, (external) but we don't have a living and longing passion for more of Jesus (internal).

We cling to what happened with God last week, last month, or last year, but can't recount anything fresh happening in us today.

God's Atomic Power is Contingent Upon an Encounter with His Spirit!

If we don't experience God's Spirit, we don't experience

God's power! If we don't have a touch of God upon our heads, all we have is empty religion.

Wait for Him!

"Behold, I send the Promise of My Father upon you; but tarry in the city of Jerusalem until you are endued with power from on high." (Luke 24:49)

Our previous experiences with God are all well and good, but we really need renewal daily. We must spend time waiting until we are clothed and endued with power from on high!

Sadly, too many believers are content to go without the power of God in their lives. It is enough for them to make it to a church service, but no more. One more sermon with lots of practical theology, but powerless.

Theory is Good, Now Go Unto the Experience!

It was the church in Ephesus that had not heard of the Holy Spirit when the Apostle Paul confronted them and asked, *Then what were you baptized into then?*

They said that they had been baptized by water for the remission of sin, but not baptized into the Spirit of God. What a difference religion is from the real experience of God!

Listen to the encounter:

"And it happened, while Apollos was at Corinth, that Paul, having passed through the upper regions, came to Ephesus. And finding some disciples he said to them, 'Did you receive the Holy Spirit when you believed?'

So they said to him, 'We have not so much as heard whether there is a Holy Spirit.'

And he said to them, 'Into what then were you baptized?'

So they said, 'Into John's baptism.'

Then Paul said, 'John indeed baptized with a baptism of repentance, saying to the people that they should believe on Him who would come after him, that is, on Christ Jesus.'

When they heard *this*, they were baptized in the name of the Lord Jesus. And when Paul had laid hands on them, the Holy Spirit came upon them, and they spoke with tongues and prophesied. Now the men were about twelve in all." (Acts 19:1-7)

The theory was fine until the experience came and verified this powerful atomic power of God in the Ephesian believers.

Never be content with the theory; never be content with a prophetic word or sermon; always seek the experience that follows them!

Neh'enah.

48

God's Atomic Power - Part 9

"Many hardships *and* perplexing circumstances confront the righteous, But the LORD rescues him from them all." (Psalm 34:19 -AMP)

One thing we all must come to grips with, is the fact that if you walk in God's atomic power, you must also endure atomic trials, persecutions, and perplexing circumstances. Does this sound familiar to you? Do you have a clue of what I am speaking of?

The facts are plain and there is no mistaking the message here: the enemy will be attracted to God's atomic power and will hate you for it, yes, till the day you die. Sounds morbid, scary, or unfair maybe, but it is what it is!

Now another fact is this: there is nothing for us to be afraid of if we stay under God's authority structure and/or umbrella of protection. We have nothing to fear if we abide in the vine, as Jesus so beautifully suggested in John 15.

In serving my King, I have experienced my share of struggle and pain and pretty much all that is in between. Yet, as the Scripture promises in Psalm 34:19, **"Many hardships and perplexing circumstances confront the righteous,**

But the LORD rescues him from them all."

One thing I have come to know: He keeps His promises!

The Devil Hates Jesus

When Jesus, the image of the invisible God, appeared on the earth, the devil recognized him right away. From the day that he heard of Jesus doing the works of God, he wanted to kill him. He tried everything in his arsenal to get it done, but nothing worked.

Finally, he gave it one last shot — he crucified him; yes, he killed Him by hanging Him on a wooden cross — the cross of Calvary!

If you remember, Jesus had announced to the whole world that in 3 days, yes in 72 hours, that He would rise again… and He did! It took Christ 3 days to dismantle the horrible work of Satan upon the earth and to establish the potential for mankind to be restored and make his way back to God.

"As He said."

"Now after the Sabbath, as the first *day* of the week began to dawn, Mary Magdalene and the other Mary came to see the tomb. And behold, there was a great earthquake; for an angel of the Lord descended from heaven and came and rolled back the stone from the door and sat

on it. His countenance was like lightning, and his cloth-
ing as white as snow. And the guards shook for fear of
him and became like dead *men*. But the angel answered
and said to the women, 'Do not be afraid, for I know that
you seek Jesus who was crucified. He is not here; for He
is risen, as He said.'"** (Matthew 28:1-6)

The Lord Himself demonstrated this atomic power by coming out of the grave in power and with great victory! Listen to Colossians 2:15: **"When He had disarmed the rulers and authorities,** (those supernatural forces of evil operating against us) **He made a public example of them,** (exhibiting them as captives in His triumphal procession) **having triumphed over them through the cross."**

Amazing Grace, how sweet the sound!

You see, the devil gave it his all, but his all wasn't enough. The devil attempted to discredit Christ, he [the devil] mocked and ridiculed Jesus daily, by bringing demons into Christ's presence and even they couldn't stop Him, then again the devil tried to accuse Jesus before Pilate, and that didn't work; the devil got the people to vote on Christ's death, to which they agreed in unison that He should die; they ridiculed Him some more before beating the *daylights* out of Him; then finally they hung Christ on a cross and pierced His side. Talk about trying to stop God!

The story doesn't end there:

After crucifying Him, they took the body of Jesus and put Him in a tomb. They put a huge stone to keep people out, they put guards to keep the disciples from coming in and stealing the body, and finally the devil waited and waited until the third day…**"And behold, there was a great earthquake; for an angel of the Lord descended from heaven, and came and rolled back the stone from the door, and sat on it."**

Here is a picture of what God thinks of **all** the works of Satan — He renders the devil, the enemy of our souls, powerless— with one little push, He simply rolls away the stones (in our lives) and sits on them! **"To him *be* glory and dominion for ever and ever. Amen."** (1 Peter 5:11)

Neh'enah.

49

God's Atomic Power – Part 10

"But you have carefully followed my doctrine, manner of life, purpose, faith, longsuffering, love, perseverance, persecutions, afflictions, which happened to me at Antioch, at Iconium, at Lystra—what persecutions I endured. And out of *them* all the Lord delivered me. Yes, and all who desire to live godly in Christ Jesus will suffer persecution." (2 Timothy 3:10-12)

In pondering these words penned by the great Apostle Paul, I can only imagine the sufferings for Christ's sake. His manner of life was lived with atomic power, and yes, the devil knew it!

For some reason the sons of Sceva come to my mind — it's a story found in Acts 19:

"Now God worked unusual miracles by the hands of Paul, so that even handkerchiefs or aprons were brought from his body to the sick, and the diseases left them, and the evil spirits went out of them. Then some of the itinerant Jewish exorcists took it upon themselves to call the name of the Lord Jesus over those who had evil spirits, saying, 'We exorcize you by the Jesus whom Paul preaches.'

Also, there were seven sons of Sceva, a Jewish chief priest, who did so. And the evil spirit answered and said, 'Jesus I know, and Paul I know; but who are you?' Then the man in whom the evil spirit was leaped on them, overpowered them, and prevailed against them, so that they fled out of that house naked and wounded."

It is very evident that the devil knew Paul. No one is more informed regarding Paul than the devil himself.

The Devil Hated Paul!

What a coincidence that wherever Paul went to speak, he was confronted by opposing forces. Either a Jewish leader, a High Priest, and even the brothers from the churches, all of them— attacked him.

Listen to some of Paul's challenges:

"Are they Hebrews? So *am* I. Are they Israelites? So *am* I. Are they the seed of Abraham? So *am* I. Are they ministers of Christ?—I speak as a fool—I *am* more: in labors more abundant, in *stripes* above measure, in prisons more frequently, in deaths often. From the Jews five times I received forty stripes minus one. Three times I was beaten with rods; once I was stoned; three times I was shipwrecked; a night and a day I have been in the deep; in journeys often, *in* perils of waters, *in* perils of robbers, *in* perils of *my own* countrymen, *in* perils of the

Gentiles, in perils in the city, in perils in the wilderness, in perils in the sea, in perils among false brethren; in weariness and toil, in sleeplessness often, in hunger and thirst, in fastings often, in cold and nakedness—besides the other things, what comes upon me daily: my deep concern for all the churches. Who is weak, and I am not weak? Who is made to stumble, and I do not burn *with indignation*? If I must boast, I will boast in the things which concern my infirmity. The God and Father of our Lord Jesus Christ, who is blessed forever, knows that I am not lying. In Damascus the governor, under Aretas the king, was guarding the city of the Damascenes with a garrison, desiring to arrest me; but I was let down in a basket through a window in the wall, and escaped from his hands." (2 Corinthians 11:22-33)

The enemy will always do his best to stop the servant of God who moves with atomic power; he will always make life complicated for that man of God.

Listen to Paul's comforting words in 2 Timothy 3, **"…what persecutions I endured. And out of *them* all the Lord delivered me."**

Even with the devil's fiery darts coming from different directions in the life of Paul, it didn't scare him, it didn't stop him, and it didn't deviate him from the Great Commission.

Neh'enah.

50

God's Atomic Power – Part 11

"If the world hates you, you know that *it hated* Me before it hated you. If you were of the world, the world would love its own. Yet because you are not of the world, but I chose you out of the world, therefore the world hates you. Remember the word that I said to you, 'A servant is not greater than his master.'

If they persecuted Me, they will also persecute you." (John 15:18-20)

One of the things that I have learned from reading the life story of Jesus in the gospels, is that although He was full of atomic power, He was also surrounded by haters! Just because you are anointed by the Lord to do His service, does not exempt the servant of God from being persecuted!

I do believe that all these haters are demonically sent by Satan himself. It is the devil's attempt to stop the life of God from being presented to the lost and dying in this world. So, for your information: If you carry the life of God within, the devil is coming after your life. If the agenda is to promote the life God gives, yes, you will be persecuted and then some!

As a matter of fact, Christ was more than just hated, He was crucified. He was killed for demonstrating the life of God, the love of the Father, and the model for kingdom living. I mean, it was a direct assault on the life God wanted for His creation!

Now, there is no need to fear, **"...because the one who is in you is greater than the one who is in the world."** (1 John 4:4).

Seriously, there is no need to fear for the atomic power of God that is within you, and will demolish every stronghold that comes against you!

The Devil Hates You!

Jesus was very clear about persecution coming to His followers. He wasn't shy about it. He told them very plainly, **"If they persecuted Me, they will also persecute you."**

Here's what we must learn...

The devil hated Jesus from the beginning. He came after Him with rage and destruction; He wasn't joking, playing games, or taunting Christ for the fun of it. No. The devil meant business and made his move.

He put Christ on a cross and hung him to die. He thought it was over. But Christ rose from the dead. Since he couldn't destroy Christ, he now comes after you and me.

His game plan is to destroy the Christian followers. He will attack by using our flesh, unleashing the world against us, or he himself makes the attempt to seduce us into something that is outside of God's will for our lives. He will attempt anything to ensnare us and destroy us.

He truly hates us and will kill us if he can.

Remember, he hated God. He hated Christ. Now, he hates you! It's time to wake up and get on with the program — the devil is not your friend!

Neh'enah.

51

God Needs to Get Us There!

"When they had twisted a crown of thorns, they put it on His head, and a reed in His right hand. And they bowed the knee before Him and mocked Him, saying, 'Hail, King of the Jews!'
Then they spat on Him and took the reed and struck Him on the head. And when they had mocked Him, they took the robe off Him, put His own clothes on Him, and led Him away to be crucified. Now as they came out, they found a man of Cyrene, Simon by name. Him they compelled to bear His cross." (Matthew 27:29-32)

This morning while I sought God in prayer, the Holy Spirit opened the eyes of my heart to see His real intent regarding these verses in Matthew 27.

The sufferings of Christ before He was to be taken to be crucified, speak about the call of God upon all who desire to live godly in Christ Jesus.

As the Apostle Paul wrote so eloquently in Philippians 3: "…that I may know Him and the power of His resurrection, and the fellowship of His sufferings, being conformed to His death, if, by any means, I may attain to the resurrection from the dead."

The Pattern!

Reading the crucifixion story and how Christ was mistreated, is just the pattern for all who desire to follow Him in this world.

Before anyone can truly consider Christ, they must be ready to die to self. It is impossible to follow God and all that He desires for us if we don't live a life of total surrender.

Some may say, *Christ had to suffer for my sake because He was the Savior of the world. He was our redeemer! Since I am not a redeemer, why should I have to suffer?"*

That is a great question, if you want to excuse yourself from living the life Christ lived! Jesus said in the book of Luke: **"Then He said to *them* all, 'If anyone desires to come after Me, let him deny himself, and take up his cross daily, and follow Me. For whoever desires to save his life will lose it, but whoever loses his life for My sake will save it.'"** (Luke 9:23, 24)

God's Way of Entering Life is Through the Cross!

As mystical as this may sound, God's way of learning is through the cross. The cross is a symbol of death; it is the method God uses to crucify our flesh. Either we live for ourselves, or we live for the Spirit of God.

If we don't carry our cross, then we don't die to our flesh. Not *dying* to self makes us selfish. Selfish people only know how to please themselves, and everything they do is for their own gain. Selfish people only know to sin!

Now if we carry our cross, the life of God can now take effect in us and through us. Therefore Luke 9:23 and 24 are so vital to the spiritual life of any believer. If we neglect these verses, we might as well forget the whole bible. Unless we die, we can't live. Unless we die to self, we can't live for God. If we don't die, God can't flow through us!

Many Obstacles to Get to the Cross!

Now, there are many things that will always prevent us from getting ourselves to the place of death. People, situations, personal preferences, conveniences, and unwillingness to die to self.

It is in God's heart to get us to the cross for the sake of our future in Him.

God Will Always Send a Helper!

In the story of Christ carrying His cross, the cross was heavy, and Christ was already weak from the previous beatings. So, the question in heaven was, *Will Christ make it to the cross, or will He faint along the way?*

Not to worry, the Lord also provided for Christ to get to His desired end by putting a man by the name of Simeon on the way. Listen to this: **"Now as they came out, they found a man of Cyrene, Simon by name. Him they compelled to bear His cross."**

When things seem like we are not going to get to the place God desires, He always provides someone or something to help get us there!

Please know that God's will is that we get on the cross daily. God will use anything to get us to the place of death. He will bring adversity at times; He will bring a friendly reminder that our lives are not our own. He will use things to offend us or make us realize that we no longer live, but Christ.

The cross of Christ is the distinguishing factor for those who truly want more of Jesus in their lives!

Neh'enah.

52

In Visions of God!

"Now it came to pass in the thirtieth year, in the fourth *month*, on the fifth *day* of the month, as I *was* among the captives by the River Chebar, *that* the heavens were opened and I saw visions of God." (Ezekiel 1:1)

While in prayer and meditation this morning, the Holy Spirit opened my eyes to this verse in Ezekiel. I was truly caught up with the vision that God allowed this man to see and deeply immerse his attention in who God is.

One of the things that I have longed for is happening as I write. I don't know how God does it, but He keeps filling my life with ideas to keep me writing and empowering others to love and serve God.

If this is what I am supposed to do with the rest of my life, I would not complain. God has been so good to me, and the way He opens my eyes to see Him is overwhelming and beautiful at the same time.

Let me show you what God showed me this morning:

As I started reading the book of Ezekiel, I took note of the time frame when Ezekiel had this vision. It was during the time of captivity when God's people were still under the Chaldean bondage (in Babylon) for the sins they had committed against God.

It was under this situation, that God came to Ezekiel with an astounding vision of Himself. As the late and powerful man of God T. Austin Sparks once wrote, *"When things have fallen and are broken— when things are beyond human repair, then God will come in with a revelation of Himself."*

Have you ever wondered why sometimes God sends us to distant places, be it spiritually, emotionally, or geographically? Why will He not deal with us right where we are at? These are great questions.

I think God sends us away because in our present state, we are not ready to listen to instruction, to wisdom, to any form of correction, etc. We need to be carried away so that we may return later in a refined way!

As difficult as these experiences may be for us and for those around us, they are necessary for our continual growth. No one knows it better than we do!

For God to take us to a difficult place is truly not a plan of His; He is only looking for a place where we can be receptive— a place where we can be focused on what He is doing.

God Has Not Forsaken You!

Here's what I did learn this morning: God will never leave us alone during a chaotic situation. Sooner or later, He will appear before us, opening the heavens and giving us visions of our future!

We will never be left alone to deal with life as an orphan left by their parents. Not God! He will always carry us through, even if we find ourselves under severe judgment! To God be the glory now and forever. Amen.

Neh'enah.

Ministry Information

Shabar Publications is a ministry expression under Masterbuilder Ministries, Inc. in Palmhurst, Texas. This publication ministry, was founded and created for the purpose of writing books and distributing them to the body of Christ both locally and globally. The intent behind the idea of publishing these works, is to train and equip the reader to be a more intimate lover of Jesus Christ, our Lord! Out of an intimate life with God, by the grace of God, effective ministry will be the outflow.

For more information regarding this ministry, feel free to email us at: mayorga1126@gmail.com.

Ministry Resources

Most Shabar Publications products are available at special quantity discounts for bulk purchase for sales promotions, fund-raising and educational needs. For details, write Shabar Publications at mayorga1126@gmail.com.

For the purchase of more books written by David Mayorga, visit our bookstore at:

www.shabarpublications.com

Volume 6

The Heart of David Journal

Volume 6

Volume 6

Volume 6

www.ingramcontent.com/pod-product-compliance
Lightning Source LLC
Chambersburg PA
CBHW020111240426
43673CB00019B/427